Haunted By The Things You Love

Haunted By The Things You Love

John Zaffis and Rosemary Ellen Guiley

Visionary Living, Inc.
New Milford, Connecticut

Haunted By The Things You Love

By John Zaffis and Rosemary Ellen Guiley

Cover design by Raúl DaSilva
Rendering and layout by Ray DaSilva
Cover photos by Elaine Snowbeck
Back jacket and interior design by Leslie McAllister

ISBN: 978-0-9860778-2-1 (pbk.)
ISBN: 978-0-9860778-1-4 (e-pub)

Published by Visionary Living, Inc.
New Milford, Connecticut
www.visionaryliving.com

Table of Contents

Introduction
By Rosemary Ellen Guiley

If you pick up an object and have an odd or uneasy feeling, it's not your imagination. Whatever you are holding has invisible secrets waiting for someone to release them. If that person is you, a personal paranormal nightmare ensues, in which you and your household are plagued by unpleasant phenomena that won't go away: poltergeist disturbances, nightmares, apparitions, shadow people, and ugly forms. In addition, there are other effects that are not obviously paranormal, but spring from the same problem: runs of bad luck, accidents, misfortunes, and illness.

Both of us, John Zaffis and myself, Rosemary Ellen Guiley, see this scenario unfold almost every day. We receive emails and calls from people who are suffering a sudden eruption of phenomena they do not understand, and, by the time they reach us, they are desperate for a solution. The cause of their problem is often an object they brought into their home. Unbeknownst to them, riding along with it was a troublesome spirit, a curse, or residues of the dead. Who would think that an ordinary item might carry such a punch? Objects both old and new can, and do.

Every day, millions of objects change hands, through selling and buying, giving and receiving, and even finding. Most of the time, nothing out of the ordinary happens. Life would be quite topsy turvy for all of us if everything we acquired came "haunted." But often enough, there's trouble.

John Zaffis has been studying and collecting haunted objects throughout his distinguished 40-year career in the paranormal and demonology, making him easily the world's leading expert on how and why inanimate things can spring to life and wreak havoc. John has created a Museum of the Paranormal to house and exhibit his collection, and this book features some of his strangest objects and the bizarre and terrifying stories behind them.

John's museum features hundreds and hundreds of objects of all kinds: ordinary household goods, clothing, jewelry, furniture, dolls, collectibles, machines and appliances, musical instruments, religious items, ritual magic items, figurines and statues, photographs, paintings and drawings, crystals and stones, pieces of architecture, and more. Any object can become haunted—there are no limits. We figure we see only the tip of the iceberg of these cases, and that an untold number, many more, go undiagnosed and unreported.

The ability of spirits to inhabit objects has been known since ancient times. People have housed and even imprisoned spirits in objects. For example, ritual masks have been made to house spirits, which bond with the wearers during ritual. Rings, jewelry, bowls, and containers have been used to capture and imprison spirits for the purpose of service, or to prevent them from causing trouble. The ancient Babylonian incantation bowl is an example of the latter, which was used to capture annoying spirits and prevent them from occupying buildings and homes. The bowl was a clay vessel inscribed with protection spells against spirits, and it was placed upside down to representation capture.

Objects can be cursed as well. Dolls called poppets, representing a victim, can be imbued with spirits who are charged with carrying out tasks, usually harm. Dolls are not the only "cursable" items, as you will see in this book. Drawings, bookends, jewelry, and figurines have made excellent Trojan horses to get a curse inside a household.

In addition, objects can take on the essence and emotions of their owners, which linger and manifest as thoughtforms, strange emotions, and even haunting phenomena.

To modern Western audiences, these concepts are superstition. They are not, as unsuspecting people from all walks of life discover on a daily basis. One need not be involved in the paranormal or occult to experience a haunted object.

John and I met more than 10 years ago, and we have consulted with and helped each other on many cases. From the beginning, I was particularly intrigued by his collection of haunted objects, because I had encountered so many cases of them myself in my 30-plus-year career in the paranormal. Early on in my paranormal study and psychic training, I learned psychometry, which is sensing the energy of things. At a subtle level, everything hums with its own energy. Objects act like sponges, absorbing the energy around them, including the energy of people. Thoughts, emotions, and even past events can become stored in an object like psychic recordings. By handling objects, a person can pick up mental impressions and information about the people who have owned or used them, and about spirit activity associated with them. This energy is well below the radar of our attention in ordinary living, but it breaks through when we are drawn to or repelled by certain objects in dramatic ways.

When we investigate hauntings, we often find that afflicted objects are a primary cause. Hauntings can be quite complex, and the human dynamics—people's emotions, activities, psychic sensitivity, personal issues, and so on—are real wild cards. Sometimes objects that have spirit attachments are dormant until they are acquired by the right person, whose activities, energy field, or home energy provide the ideal ingredients for activation. Thus, it is not unusual for one person in a household to be the focal point, while others experience little or even nothing.

John explored many of these scenarios in his hit reality show on the *SyFy* channel, *Haunted Collector*. I appeared on two episodes involving problematic Ouija boards. I have also featured haunted objects in some of the books I have written.

We have discussed ideas for this book for several years, and we are delighted to bring forth this extraordinary collection of riveting stories, as well as educational information about the paranormal. We selected a representation of the wide variety of items and haunting circumstances. Not only do we tell each story, we analyze the how and why of it. In addition, we provide a detailed explanation of the ways in which objects become haunted; the types of energies and beings involved; and advice on how to deal with such objects. You will also learn about John's unique background that led to the John Zaffis Museum of the Paranormal.

The stories are real, taken straight out of John's case files. For the privacy of the people involved, we have used pseudonyms and have obscured or changed personal details. We have recreated scenes and dialogue for drama. Many cases involve thorough investigations conducted by John's team to document activity and determine other causes of phenomena. With one exception ("Possessed Mirrors"), we have not included the details of investigations in order to streamline the stories and keep the focus on the haunted objects. We have not included photographs of the objects for privacy reasons, and in some cases we have altered details about the objects for the same reasons. John's website, www.johnzaffis.com, has a tour of the Museum of the Paranormal that features photos.

xii HAUNTED BY THE THINGS YOU LOVE

I have had many cases similar to John's and throughout the book I have contributed to the analyses of the cases, and provided supporting material.

Haunted By The Things You Love will open your eyes to another level of reality. You may never shop the same again.

1

Creepy Clown Dolls Take Over

The nightmares were happening almost every night: Sarah was in a dark and alien landscape, running from distorted black shadow figures who shape-shifted into monsters with leering, clown-like faces sporting huge red lips that parted to reveal rows of saw teeth. The nightmare always ended the same way, with Sarah jerking violently awake just as the monsters closed in.

Alone in bed, she sat up and clutched the covers to her chin. Her heart was racing and her skin felt clammy. It took a few minutes to reorient to her room. Even though she was relieved to be out of the nightmare, her surroundings gave her little comfort. There was a weird energy in the air, and in the darkness her furniture and things looked oddly distorted. Once again, she knew that somehow these repeating nightmares—as well as other strange activity in the house—had to do with the new clown dolls. Ever since she had added them to her collection, she had been plunged into an eerie reality where "normal" no longer ruled.

She didn't want to look, but she had to know. Were the dolls in their places—or not?

Sarah slowly got out of bed and reached for her robe. The door to her bedroom was open, and the shadowy hallway lay beyond it. She turned on a hall light and padded out through the living room to a small study that opened on one side. There Sarah had on display dozens of her prized clown dolls, many from limited editions.

She knew what she would see even before she turned on the study light. Yes. Once again, the two new dolls were not where she had put them, tucked into their own special spot on a shelf. One was on the floor in a corner of the room. Its little boy friendly face with an open red mouth seemed now to leer at her. The other doll, with the face of a little girl, was resting on top of the heads of two of her other dolls.

A pang of nausea swept through Sarah. She didn't want to touch them.

This had to stop. *I'm calling John Zaffis in the morning,* she resolved. She spent the rest of the night with all the lights on in her house.

John received a call from Sarah the next day about mid-morning. She introduced herself and explained that she had gotten his name and number from an acquaintance "who knows about these things"—meaning strange phenomena that belonged in a scary movie, not in someone's comfortable suburban home. Sarah told John about the dolls and the nightmares and a host of other events that had no natural explanation. He booked an appointment to see her that evening.

John was greeted by a middle-aged woman with short brown hair. She was neatly dressed in casual clothes and makeup. Her jewelry said that she liked fine things. He always took note of a person's appearance—it said a lot about their emotional and mental states, which are often factors in paranormal activity. Sarah looked well grounded.

John had seen lots of collections of all kinds of things, but was astonished at the size of Sarah's clown doll collection. Every nook and cranny in her special room for them was filled with clown dolls of all sizes. Some were obviously made for collectors and others were old and worn children's toys. Sarah gave John the clown doll tour, explaining where she had gotten various ones and why they were special. Some were quite valuable. Some had happy faces, some sad. Some looked surprised. There were no "killer" clown faces, however.

"I've been fascinated by clowns ever since I was a kid," Sarah said. "The first time my dad took me to see the circus, I was mesmerized by the clowns."

Sarah explained that about two months earlier, she had been browsing in an antiques and collectibles shop and had found five clown dolls from a highly prized limited edition. She bought two of them, a boy and a girl, and was so pleased to add them to her collection.

"That's them there," she said, pointing to them. Her voice suddenly quivered. "That's where I found them last night. I didn't want to move them. They should be on this shelf here"—she pointed to a bookcase with an empty spot—"but they just won't stay there. I keep putting them there, and they—they *move*."

John picked the dolls up. They both had yellowish-green faces carefully painted in red and white. One had an open mouth, as though it was about to laugh or speak. It was dressed in a blue and yellow striped shirt, contrasting pinstriped trousers and bowtie, red suspenders fastened with black buttons, and black shoes. A cap matching the trousers framed tufts of orange hair. The red lips were surrounded by white, and the button black eyes had wide white ovals around them, giving the clown a bright-eyed look. There were red eyebrows, a red ball nose, blue diamonds on the cheeks, and a blue diamond in the center of the forehead.

The second doll had a more serious or sad look. Its eyes were at half-mast, and its mouth was closed, though the small lips had a slight curve to them. A big red ball formed the nose. Yellow hair showed beneath a red striped cap that matched the jacket. The trousers were red and white checks. A red scarf was tied around its neck. It had the same black shoes as its companion. Both of them had little white hands.

The dolls were in excellent condition, and at first glance, one would never suspect them of being anything more than... *dolls*.

John could usually tell by looking at an object and by touching it whether it had a spirit problem. These certainly did. While he was handling them, he saw out of the corner of his eye a dark shadow figure slide quickly across the room on his left side. He kept quiet and let Sarah finish her story. He didn't want to alarm her.

"As soon as I brought them home, the atmosphere in the house changed," Sarah said. "I didn't think anything of it at the time, but now I think it was significant."

"How did it change?" John asked. He already knew the answer—this was falling into a pattern he saw over and over again.

Sarah hunched her shoulders and folded her arms. "Chilly. I've lived here by myself for nine years now, since my divorce. This house has always been so bright and friendly. But after the dolls came, it has a coldness to it, if you know what I mean."

John nodded.

"Like I said, I didn't make much of it, and I certainly didn't think it had anything to do with the dolls," she went on. "Other than that, everything was fine for a few days, and then I started noticing odd things. I would walk into a room and a light would be on, when I knew I hadn't left it on. Sometimes I would leave a light on and then find it off.

"I would hear strange noises. Rustling sounds, like something moving around. At first I thought maybe I had mice, or there were squirrels in the attic, but I don't have either one. When I would go to bed, I would hear tapping on the walls. It would start on one wall and go all the way around. I knew it couldn't be the house settling. House noises don't go around a room.

"Then the dolls started moving. I would walk into the room and find them in different places. No one lives here but me. No one comes in while I'm away. *How on earth can dolls just up and move themselves?*" Her voice rose.

"I'll tell you what is going on in a minute," John said. "But first tell me what else has happened."

"That really upset me, the dolls moving," Sarah said. "Once or twice, I thought maybe I was absent-minded and just forgot that I had shifted them around. But I don't move the dolls except to clean, and then I put them back. Each one has its own place." She looked at John helplessly.

"Everything started to increase," Sarah said. "The sounds, the lights, the dolls moving. I got the feeling the dolls *knew* they were upsetting me— like they were alive. Then the nightmares started about two weeks ago." She shivered. "Every night, the same dream." She described the pursuit by shadowy monsters. "I'm not crazy, am I?"

John smiled. "Of course not. But I do think you have a paranormal issue. Sometimes spirit energy gets attached to objects. It may come from previous owners, or from places where they were kept. There are many reasons why it can happen. The good news is, we can do something about it. First I need to get some more information about the dolls."

John got the name and address of the collectibles shop where Sarah had purchased the dolls, and said he would pay a call there and get more information on them. He told her it would be a good idea to remove them from the house in the meantime. With her permission, he took them out to the garage.

The shop owner was not at all pleased to talk to John. "I don't believe in the paranormal," she huffed.

"I'm not here to convince you, I'd like to get some information so that I can help this lady," John said.

She told him the dolls had come from a woman who had a large collection of this particular limited edition. She did not know how many dolls the client had, but she had been willing to take five of them on consignment in the shop. They had sold right away: two to Sarah, two to another woman, and one to a third woman. She declined to refer John to the original owner, or the other two purchasers.

"That's all I know," she said curtly. Then she blurted out, "I was always creeped out about those clowns. I will never have clowns in my shop again!" The glare she shot John conveyed in no uncertain terms that he should leave and not come back.

He thanked her and left. Actually, she had confirmed all of John's impressions that he had obtained from Sarah's dolls when he saw them and picked them up.

Several days after his visit with Sarah, John phoned her to get an update. She told him that since the dolls had been placed in the garage, the house had been quiet. "I haven't had any nightmares, either," she said. She paused and added emphatically, "I don't want them in the house again. Should I get rid of them?"

"I'll take them off your hands," he said. "I know just what to do with them."

"They won't come back, will they? Like one of those horror movies? I feel silly asking, but…" her voice trailed off.

"I'll make sure they don't," he assured her.

The next day John returned to Sarah's home. The atmosphere had changed dramatically. It felt "quiet." She seemed less ruffled and on edge.

"The clown dolls you bought definitely have spirit energy attached to them," he told her.

She looked like John had confirmed her worst fears. "Demons?"

He shook my head. "No, not everything is a demon. These dolls have spirit energy. There are different kinds. The previous owner might have had a very strong emotional bond to the dolls. If he or she didn't want to sell the collection, or see the collection get broken up, some of that emotional attachment can go with the dolls. The energy takes on a personality and starts activity to get attention.

"Another kind of energy is an actual spirit who gets attracted to an object and attaches itself to it like a home. It rides around with the object, and it might even be dormant and quiet for a long time. Then it gets into a place where the energy is right, and it wakes up and starts activity. Depending on the kind of spirit, things can escalate and get nasty. There are spirits who look for attention, and who feed off people by making them frightened. They use our emotional energy like gasoline."

"Is it attached to me?" Sarah asked, concern in her eyes.

"No, or the activity would have kept up even with the dolls in the garage, and it would have followed you when you went outside your house. All the activity stayed here."

John recommended to Sarah that she call in a minister or spiritual person to bless and cleanse the house to get rid of residual energy, which can cling to a place like dusty cobwebs. She agreed to do that right away.

He retrieved the dolls from the garage and took them home. Outside, he treated them with sea salt and holy water, and said special prayers over them. He let them sit outside for several days while they neutralized and cleansed. Then he brought them inside and repeated the procedure, and performed a ritual for binding the spirits to the dolls. They joined the John Zaffis Museum of the Paranormal, the premier collection of haunted objects from all over the world. The haunted items are responsible for all kinds of paranormal mayhem, including possession.

John has more dolls than any other kind of "paranormal problem" object, and of the dolls, the majority of them are clown dolls. What is it about dolls, and especially clown dolls, that goes haywire and starts a haunting?

Dolls are among the best targets for spirit activity. They are like miniature people, and when children play with them, they animate the dolls and give them personalities with their imagination. Adults relate to them in the same way.

Sometimes people use dolls in magic and spell-casting rituals. They are substitutes for the person who is the object of a spell. In such cases, spirits are summoned and lodged in the dolls. John believed that the previous owner of Sarah's dolls was doing something occult with the entire collection.

Clowns have another aspect when it comes to hauntings. Many people are terrified of clowns. They may look happy or sad, and their purpose may be to amuse in silly ways, but underneath their masks lurks the unknown. Many psychologists have analyzed clown fears and phobias. In our subconscious, we know that the clown is really unpredictable. The pasted-on face of wild makeup may hide something dark and sinister— which horror novelists like Stephen King have made use of in their tales of terror. In King's *It*, the sadistic clown Pennywise is actually a supernatural killer. And who can forget the demonic faces of the alien clowns in the movie *Killer Klowns from Outer Space*?

The clown doll or creepy doll that comes to life at night is a staple in horror. In an early episode of *The Twilight Zone*, a doll named Talking Tina takes a distinct dislike to the hostile stepfather of a little girl who loves the doll. "My name is Talking Tina and I don't like you," the doll warns him. He tries in vain to destroy the doll, but it won't cut or burn, and it moves on its own. "My name is Talking Tina and I'm going to kill you," it says. The doll makes good on its promise by luring the man out into the hall at night—where he trips over it and makes a fatal plunge down the stairs.

John had yet to see a real-life killer doll, but he had seen plenty of dolls that caused a great deal of paranormal havoc.

It always interested John why so many people unconsciously chose dolls that came loaded with spirit energy, rather than dolls that were non-energetic. Like Sarah, some were collectors, and their emotional high at adding a "find" to their collection probably canceled out any warning from their intuition. With others, it was often a moth to flame story. Some people were unconsciously drawn to the paranormal. If there was a haunted object available, they managed to find it, usually without realizing it. Their problems then ranged from mild hauntings to life-threatening possessions and take-overs.

One of the clown dolls at the John Zaffis Museum of the Paranormal is nicknamed the "Evil Clown." Visitors find the doll disturbing even to look at. On the surface it looks like an ordinary clown doll. Look long enough and it seems to be surrounded by a dark energy. Maybe its unsettling appearance is what attracted a young college student to buy it as a weird birthday present for his girlfriend.

John acquired the Evil Clown at a college in the Midwest where he was lecturing about some of his cases. After his presentation, a young woman student came up and told him about the doll. She and her friends were amused by the appearance of the clown and thought it was cool. It was a novelty item for their dorm room. In the days that followed, the student and her roommate noticed strange occurrences in their room. They had the constant feeling of being watched, as well as persistent headaches and nausea. If they took the doll out of the room, the phenomena stopped.

The doll was moved around from dorm room to dorm room. Wherever it went, the occupants experienced the same troubling activity. Finally all the girls decided to get rid of it, and they tossed the clown out into the hallway. Later it was found at the bottom of a staircase by a hall monitor, who, thinking someone had lost it, took it to the counselor's office for safekeeping.

Meanwhile, the students went to the counselor to discuss the clown doll and their fears about it. The skeptical counselor was not sure what to believe, but agreed to keep the doll in her closet.

The counselor evidently got a good dose of strange, because when John paid a call at her office, she was jumpy. She urged him to take it away, but when he asked to see the doll, she froze and refused to take him to it. "I don't want anything to do with that awful thing!" she exclaimed. She insisted nothing unusual had happened in her office, but she was completely rattled. John had to have someone from campus security fetch the doll, which was stored in a canvas bag in the closet.

John never learned the back story on the Evil Clown. Sometimes it is impossible to track a historical record. The activity stirred up by haunted objects follows patterns, however.

Objects do not have to be old and secondhand to be haunted. Brand new objects can come home with a supernatural bang. That was the case with another doll in the museum, the Blue Clown, a small doll that came from the collection of a woman. Usually this woman looked for antique and unusual clowns, but she spied this one in a store, new, and decided to add it to her collection.

A short time after bringing the clown into her home, she had the uneasy feeling that it was staring at her. At times she "heard" it laughing inside her head, as though it was mocking her. Another trick this clown performed on its own was turning itself around so that its back faced out into the room.

After enduring these torments for about a week, the woman lost her temper and scolded the clown. This did not sit well with the doll, for when she turned to leave the room, she felt something hit her on the back. On the floor behind her was the doll, as though it had hurled itself across the room. She was so frightened that she called John immediately, even though it was late at night. John agreed to come and get the doll the next evening, but she could not wait. She brought it to him, along with its packaging.

Blue Clown is now neutralized in the museum. The box was new and had not been tampered with when the woman purchased the doll. How did it acquire an ill-tempered spirit? We will never know. The doll could have picked up energy from people who handled the box in the store, or even from the store environment itself, which might have had some invisible lodgers looking for new homes.

Meanwhile, another chapter unfolded in the saga of the creepy clown dolls.

A few weeks after John resolved Sarah's haunting, the second woman who bought two of the "special" limited edition clown dolls found him. She was having problems, too.

Rhonda collected many kinds of dolls besides clowns. At the time of her purchase of the two clowns, she had also gotten a third doll from the same shop. She described to John the same problems that had plagued Sarah: shadow figures flitting about the house, poltergeist activity that escalated, and terrifying nightmares that repeated.

"The clowns are coming after me in the dreams," she said. "It's really them—the ones from the shop! I have this feeling that wherever I go, they will find me!"

The third doll was benign, but the two clown dolls moved around on their own. They did not limit themselves to the room where they were placed for display. Rhonda found them all over the house. She would come home from work and one would be sitting on the bathroom sink. She opened her pantry and there would be a clown doll, leering out at her. Even worse, she would find one sitting on her bed.

"Stop it! Stop it!" she screamed at them, but her anger only made things worse. She even threw them in the garbage—but they made their way back into the house.

"I thought about taking them to the dump," she said. "But then I was afraid that if the dolls were hurt, they would hurt me. I don't know anything about the paranormal. It doesn't make any sense. None of this should be happening!"

It made complete sense to John.

He gave her similar recommendations: Remove the dolls from the house, and get a religious or spiritual cleansing and blessing done for both the house and herself. The spirits that were attached to these two dolls were stronger than those linked to Sarah's dolls. He knew he would have to perform a cleansing and binding on them while they were still on Rhonda's property.

The clowns looked almost identical to the boy and girl clowns purchased by Sarah. There were small differences in the facial expressions and differences in the clothing. After John had treated them outdoors with sea salt, holy water and prayers, he got a surprise from Rhonda: She did not want to give the dolls up.

"They're a limited edition that is hard to find and valuable," she said. "Now that you've taken care of whatever is attached to them, isn't it okay to bring them back in the house? How could they bother me now?"

He could tell from her expression and body language that she was going to be stubborn about it. "It's not a good idea to keep them," he said. "The binding works as long as the dolls are not disturbed. If they are handled, the binding could break and then you would have the same activity start up again."

"I'll tell anyone who comes over not to touch them," she said.

"Is keeping them really worth your peace of mind? Look what's happened in a short period of time."

"I'll think about it," she said. "Thank you for your help."

John left, fully expecting that he would hear from Rhonda again within a week. She wasn't the first person to change her mind about keeping haunted objects. Anyone who did usually regretted their second thoughts because the paranormal activity always resumed, usually worse, and then could not get rid of the objects fast enough.

He did not hear from Rhonda again. As for the dolls, they probably either made a final journey to the dump—or they went to another consignment shop. Yes, it happens—recycled haunted objects.

The tale of the five dolls has one more chapter. The fifth doll surfaced with the same M.O. The woman who bought it sent John an email and a photo. It was larger than the other four, and wore a red and gold outfit with a matching pointed hat topped by a green ball. Matching balls went down the front of the outfit, and a black satin ruff was at the neck. The lips on this doll were pursed, as though it kept a secret.

The woman said she felt an evil presence was attached to the clown and it followed her from room to room in her house. She was constantly watched. She glimpsed dark shadows moving about, especially at night, and strange tapping noises sounded in unoccupied parts of the house.

John made an appointment with her, but before the date he came home one day and found a box sitting on his doorstep. It contained the doll and a note that read, "I want to get rid of this NOW. I don't want it in my house and I don't want you here either, talking about it and stirring things up."

That's the way things go sometimes—people get scared that talking and thinking about spirits will bring them back in.

They are right. It can and does happen. When we get tangled up in the spirit world, the rules of this world fly out the window.

2

The John Zaffis Museum of the Paranormal

The John Zaffis Museum of the Paranormal collection of haunted objects is the product of an extraordinary career. John had a rare introduction to the mysteries of the paranormal, schooled by two of the most famous people in the business: Ed and Lorraine Warren. Ed was John's blood uncle, a man steeped in knowledge about spirits, ghosts, and demons. His wife, Lorraine, John's aunt, possessed an exceptional clairvoyant ability. Together, the Warrens made international headlines investigating sensational demonic cases. Ed passed on in 2006, and Lorraine still lectures. Their cases have been the subjects of best-selling books, documentaries, and hit films.

Paranormal career

From an early age, John was fascinated by the paranormal, even though his mother, Babette Miney Zaffis Warren—Ed's twin sister—shied away from it (Ed's birth name was Warren Edward Miney, and he adopted Ed Warren as his professional name). John was psychically sensitive, and had startling experiences as a teen, such as a dramatic bedside visit from his deceased grandfather, who appeared as a harbinger of the death of John's grandmother.

John studied and learned from Ed and Lorraine, and when he was 18, Ed invited him to participate in their investigations. John had firsthand experience in all kinds of cases, including hauntings and intense and difficult demonic possessions. He worked with some of the most influential investigators, demonologists, and exorcists in the field. He learned about "the Work"—dealing with the demonic—a path that was fraught with danger, as Ed emphasized repeatedly. Those who attempted to interfere with and stop the forces of darkness were constantly at risk of having the evil turned against them, too, and even against their families. Few people had the mettle to stay in the Work.

One of the Warrens' cases brought John face to face with evil in a heart-stopping moment that he will never forget. The case involved a family living in a house in Southington, Connecticut that had once been a funeral home. One son was seriously ill with Hodgkins' disease. Unbeknownst to the family when they bought the house, a dark force polluted it. Phenomena began as soon as they moved in and grew steadily worse until all the family members were terrified.

The activity became so intense that the family took to sleeping together on mattresses in the living room to avoid anyone being alone at night. When the Warrens were called in, they set up round-the-clock monitoring.

One night John stayed up by himself, going over his research notes. Suddenly the temperature plunged and the room became frigid. He had a sensation that something bad was about to happen. Turning and looking up toward a staircase, he saw a murky-colored reptilian form materialize at the top of the stairs and descend rapidly toward him. Behind it were fluttering movements.

The entity said aloud in a rumbling voice, "You know what they did to us."

John was so shaken that he grabbed his car keys and exited the house. It took him three days to return, during which he withdrew from the Work and questioned his involvement in it.   He ultimately concluded that there are people who need help in dealing with the demonic, and he could not retire from the Work at any cost. As for the funeral home, it required a full exorcism by Roman Catholic clergy. The family was eventually freed from the demonic grip.

The story was told in a best-selling book, *In A Dark Place,* by the Warrens; the husband and wife involved, Al and Carmen Snedeker; and writer Ray Gorton. In 2009, the story was the basis for the film *The Haunting in Connecticut.*

John's decision to remain involved in the Work shaped the rest of his life. Today he is regarded as one of the most knowledgeable, reliable, and straightforward professionals in the paranormal. He is known affectionately as "the Godfather of the Paranormal." His expertise, especially concerning haunted objects, led to a highly successful television series on the SyFy channel, *Haunted Collector,* which ran for three seasons from 2011-2013. John starred in the series, and was a producer of the final season. Principal cast members included John's son and daughter, Christopher Zaffis and Aime'e Zaffis; Brian J. Cano; Beth Ezzo (season one); Jason J. Gates (seasons two and three); and Jesslyn Brown (seasons two and three).

The Work has its ongoing hazards, and anyone who is involved in the dark side of the paranormal must keep up a constant guard, including John. Even so, barriers are breached. Phenomena outbreaks occur from time to time in John's house, especially when he takes on a new case. In fact, sometimes he gets advance warning of a new case by the change in the atmosphere, and by activity such as the lights turning on and off by themselves and tapping on the walls. He has frequent interference on the phone when talking to victims, and problems with his computer.

When John makes a visit to a haunted site, he sometimes will be tapped on the head by invisible entities, or even bear-hugged, both personal signs of certain kinds of spirit presences. Car problems are frequent, too, especially traveling to and from a case, and transporting haunted objects home. John has had clergy bless his car to keep it protected.

The interference is annoying, but it does not approach what many of the victims experience in a problem haunting. John, as well as others who are engaged in the Work, could not function without good protection and barriers.

John has witnessed or assisted at more than 85 exorcisms, and has investigated thousands of hauntings of all kinds. The John Zaffis Museum of the Paranormal is an outgrowth of that work.

Creation of the museum

The Warrens had a collection of haunted objects from many of their cases. As John branched out into his own independent work, he continually found haunted objects behind the causes of many spirit-related troubles. What was more, most people wanted him to take their afflicted objects away, and so John's own collection was born.

Over the years, more and more items were acquired, filling the entire basement of John's home. Visitors were boggled that below the family living quarters was a stash of once horribly haunted items that had driven some victims to the brink of breakdown and insanity—and yet John and his family lived and slept peacefully above them.

"How can you stand it?" visitors would say. "Don't you ever worry about anything getting loose?" It was hard for people to grasp that John did a thorough job of clearing objects and bolting down spirits through binding.

In 1998, John formed his own organization, the Paranormal Research Society of New England, and assembled teams of investigators to handle requests for help. His right-hand associates are Larry Elward, who met John when he started investigating with the Warrens in 1985, and Larry's wife, Debbie Elward, a clairvoyant and psychic. Larry, a seminary graduate in esoteric Christianity, was ordained a priest in 2004.

The investigations brought in many more haunted objects, and soon they were spilling out of the basement. John built a separate facility for them on his property, which also houses his office. That building is now stuffed to the brim, too. Among the objects are famous ones, such as artifacts from the Southington funeral parlor case where John was confronted by the reptilian demonic entity.

John formally created the John Zaffis Museum of the Paranormal in 2004 with the intent of educating investigators, researchers, and the public about the paranormal. As of this writing, the museum is not open to the public and has no regular hours, but is open by arrangement on a limited basis. Many paranormal investigators have toured the collection. In the future, John may be able to open a public facility. He gives frequent lectures about the museum and its most unusual items.

How the objects are processed

Before items are brought into the museum, John performs binding rituals over them. The binding ends the paranormal phenomena and contains any spirits that are attached. The majority of items are in open display and can be handled. The most problematic ones that had attachments by powerful spirits are placed under acrylic containers to prevent people from touching them. Handling, says John, can disturb or even break the spiritual binding that is in place. If an item must be removed from its container, even temporarily, a binding ritual is performed again on it.

Every now and then, John comes across a haunted object that resists cleansing and binding. The spirit energy attached to it is too strong. Those items are not admitted to the museum, but are buried or thrown into deep water.

Activity at the museum

Sometimes the Museum of the Paranormal seems like a real-life version of the 2006 film, *Night At the Museum*, in which the exhibits come to life at night. Even though the objects have been treated, occasionally something gets loose and boomerangs around. It is possible, notes John, for objects to become active again, though on a much lower scale.

Visitors have sensed presences and have captured EVPs, or Electronic Voice Phenomena. EVPs are mystery voices that manifest on audio recordings, and are a staple of paranormal investigations. The voices are not heard in the environment, only on playback of a recording.

Once Rosemary and John were going through the museum collection to select and discuss items for this book. She had her digital recorder on for note-taking. When she played it back, a masculine mystery voice popped in right at the end, whispering dramatically, "John" in a long, drawn out manner.

Sometimes people hear faint but audible voices and other sounds, like shuffling steps or taps on the walls.

The objects themselves give off vibes, striking creepy notes with visitors.

John is often asked if merely seeing and being around the objects can adversely affect people. "It's very uncommon," he says, "but the potential exists. People have different sensitivities to the spirit world. Being in the museum, like doing any kind of paranormal or spirit work, has its risks."

John also is often asked which object is the worst and most dangerous in the museum. Without hesitation, his answer is, "The Idol. I still get the worst feeling from it. The black magic rituals that were associated with it were particularly disturbing, and nearly led to a young man's destruction."

3

Terror in the Idol

Kevin plunged down the stairs from his bedroom as though the devil himself were after him. Maybe it was. If not the devil, then it was something very powerful and very evil.

He stumbled into the family room where his parents were watching television. He was crying hysterically. "Mom, Dad," he gasped. "I think I brought something in! It's trying to kill me!"

His parents stared at him, too stunned for words. They had no idea what he was talking about. After a long moment of silence save for Kevin's sobbing, they jumped up and pandemonium broke loose. What unfolded stretched their belief systems to the breaking point.

Kevin led them upstairs to his bedroom. He was 16, and for months his bedroom had been his private lair. So private that he kept the door locked and allowed no one, not even his parents, inside. His parents, Tom and Christine, were liberal-minded and decided to let him have his space. He had always been a good kid, excelling in school and holding down a job. He did not hang out with troublemakers. He was a model teen, at least up until about six weeks earlier when an inexplicable change took over him.

He acquired an unkempt appearance, skipped class, lost interest in his job and quit. His appetite was off and he lost weight. Still, they thought it was "just a phase" and let it ride.

Now Tom and Christine were staring into the portals of hell.

Kevin's room no longer looked like a teenage boy's room, but like a ritual chamber in an occult movie. The curtains were drawn and black fabric draped everything, giving the room a funereal look. Lit black candles guttered and cast weird shadows. The floor was littered with unknown objects: goblets, small knives, pictures of demonic looking faces, and strange symbols. Against one wall was a small table filled with statues, papers full of symbols, and more candles. Looming over them was a large black resin head with red rimmed eyes, mounted on a pedestal. The head was misshapen and distorted. The top was unformed, to imitate a carving from rough stone. The face was long and narrow, with ugly, large ears. A moustache and beard framed a huge, drooping, open mouth.

The head looked like something straight out of someone's nightmare. Tom and Christine had never seen the head before and were horrified by it.

Kevin pointed to the head with a shaking finger. "There's something evil living inside the head," he cried, breaking out into tears again. "I can't get rid of it!"

The parents pulled the story out of him in pieces. A few weeks earlier, Kevin browsed through a yard sale on his way home from school and spied the head. It was so ugly that he thought it was cool, and he bought it for a dollar. He put it in his room without his parents ever seeing it. Initially, the head was only an object of curiosity. But a presence came along with it, and it quickly filled Kevin's room. Suddenly he had the urge to investigate magical rituals and spells, an interest he had never had before.

He researched on the net and bought magical textbooks and ritual tools. He transformed a small table into an altar and gave the head center place. He began experimenting with magic, starting with simple spells. At first nothing happened, and he quickly concluded that magic was "a bunch of bull--." Then he tried more complex rituals for summoning spirits. It became an obsession. More and more, Kevin kept to himself, both at home and at school. He put a lock on his bedroom door and spent hours inside. He never talked about what he was doing.

Rituals to summon spirits are serious business. They send calls out into the spirit world. In some cases, rituals are done badly and nothing answers, and the effort fails. In other cases, the call is answered—swiftly. Amateurs such as Kevin do not understand what they might summon, and they seldom know how to close the door to the spirit world once it opens.

Suddenly Kevin knew that he had succeeded in calling in a spirit, and it lodged itself in the idol head to hide itself. It abruptly "happened." There was no grand manifestation, no Hollywood theatrics. It was suddenly *there*. It did not leave. Kevin had the urge to paint the head to resemble what he sensed in the spirit, and he outlined the eyes in red.

Novices in the occult always think they will keep the upper hand with spirits. They often get a rude shock when the spirits abruptly turn the tables and take control. It happens frequently, and even experienced occultists can wind up in trouble.

Kevin soon found himself in deep trouble. Inky shadows moved around his room, especially at night. He heard and felt the spirit in his head, whether he wanted to or not. He could not make it go away. It watched him in his room, and its invisible eyes followed him at school, at work, everywhere.

He consulted his magical books and learned that one must demand a spirit's name in order to maintain control. In magic, a name is the true essence of any being. He demanded the spirit's name, but all he ever heard in response was gibberish, something he could not pronounce. Sounding it out phonetically did not help either—he could not find anything similar in any of his dictionaries of spirits and demons. Sometimes the spirit would say, "You know who I am," and break into hysterical laughter.

Soon the mystery spirit was telling Kevin what to do. It controlled his thoughts. Sometimes Kevin thought it controlled what he said to other people. The messages got darker. "You're worthless, go kill yourself," it said to him. "Get up on the roof and throw yourself off." Sometimes it would tell Kevin to run out into traffic and kill himself by getting hit by a car. "You deserve to die, so die now! Nobody likes you. Your parents hate you." The urge to kill himself became stronger and stronger.

Kevin quickly slid into deep depression. He stopped practicing magic rituals, but the spirit did not leave. He could not avoid its growling voice and its insistent demands to commit suicide. He tried desperately to send the spirit away, but it was strong and resistant. In fact, trying to banish it seemed to give it more strength than ever.

Finally Kevin confessed everything to his parents.

Tom and Christine did not know what to do. Suddenly they were faced with a problem that seemed completely unreal to them. Demons? Spirits in ugly idol heads? Rituals and black magic? A son possessed? These things do not happen in everyday life in a secure and peaceful suburban community.

They were not regular church goers, but they had contacts, and called in a minister. They also called John Zaffis. He got there as soon as possible.

The photograph of Kevin that was proudly displayed on the living room fireplace mantle did not match the youth he met. The Kevin in the photo looked happy and vibrant, full of life as only teens can express. He had curly dark hair that framed his handsome face nicely, and his brown eyes sparkled.

The Kevin John met looked thin and shrunken. His hair was dirty and his clothes hung on him. There were dark circles beneath his eyes, which had lost their spark and looked dull and empty.

Kevin took John up to his room. It was indeed no longer a bedroom, but an occult chamber. He had collected quite a few books on magic, demons and spirit summoning. John recognized many of the books—they were heavy duty manuals of magic. There were all sorts of ritual objects that had symbols scratched into them, something Kevin had done himself to customize them.

The idol head confirmed to John his suspicions that it had been used in ritual summoning before, and probably had been made for that purpose—an ideal house for spirits. Kevin had fumbled around until he finally managed to call in a very powerful spirit, possibly a demon, which was now in the process of possessing him.

Kevin was consumed by fear. "I've done something bad, haven't I?" he said. "Will it ever go away? Am I doomed?"

John gave him a reassuring smile. "Not doomed by a long shot, Kevin. You made a mistake, and mistakes can be fixed." He sighed and inwardly thought, *Let's hope it's fixed quickly.* Success would depend on how strong Kevin could be. It was a lot to ask of a teen.

Tom and Christine were apologetic. They felt they had failed their son in some way.

"Let's not worry about that now," John said. "Let's get this thing out of here."

Christine told John that since Kevin had revealed his activities, she had seen him "go under," that is, go into trance. Trance happens in possession cases, where the occupying spirit takes control of a person and causes them to act and speak in bizarre ways. The victim's eyes roll back and the whites look milky and covered with a film. In the worst cases, victims have seizure-like convulsions, scream obscenities, vomit, and have supernormal strength. The spirit talks through them, and their voices and even faces change dramatically.

When Kevin was "under," Christine said, he would laugh in a low, gravelly voice and talk in gibberish.

"Does it sound like a foreign language?" John asked.

She nodded. "Nothing recognizable, but it sounds like a mix of Latin and an ancient Middle Eastern tongue."

That was another sign of demonic possession. "We need a deliverance," John said. "And the name of this spirit." Knowing the name would be the first step in regaining the upper hand.

John consulted with the minister chosen by the family to perform a deliverance, a type of exorcism in which a spirit is cast out and banished. Deliverances are similar to the formal rites of exorcism practiced by the Catholic Church—they are performed by Protestant or other Christian denominations. The movies have popularized the Catholic rites, but all methods can be equally effective. In many cases, it takes more than one session to dislodge a spirit.

In the meantime, Christine took Kevin to a psychiatrist for evaluation. John usually recommends this to cover all the bases—you have to look at natural factors and explanations first before you address the supernatural.

The psychiatrist gave Kevin a clean bill of health. He was psychologically sound. That would work in his favor. Sometimes spirits latch onto people who have medical conditions or weaknesses that make it harder to get them out.

At an arranged time, John reconvened with the family and the minister. The minister brought with him a group from his church to perform prayers throughout the house. He stationed them all over: in the basement, the ground floor, upstairs, and, of course, in Kevin's room where the deliverance was done.

Kevin was seated in a hardback chair with two people from the church, one on either side, to hold onto him for support, and also to prevent the spirit from using his body to lash out. You never know how a deliverance is going to go. Sometimes the spirits leave easily, and sometimes they put up quite a fight.

The church people seated in the room began murmuring their prayers, heads bowed and hands clasped on their knees. Simultaneously, throughout the house, the other pray-ers went to work. The deliverance began. Kevin went "under" quickly—his eyes rolled back to show that milky white that identifies the presence of a spirit. The atmosphere in the room changed dramatically. It was suddenly bone-chilling cold.

The minister opened with a formal prayer and then demanded, "What is your name, spirit?"

Kevin's face contorted into a twisted grin as he spit out gibberish.

"What is your *name?*"

Again, the same, with more emphasis, followed by "Stupid!"

The minister asked several times for the name, always with the same response. John realized then that they were getting the name the spirit decided to use, but it was a tongue-twister. This was a spirit very high up in the hierarchy of power, who knew it did not have to reveal itself or prove itself. They would have to pronounce it as they heard it.

The minister informed the spirit that it was not welcome and was to depart Kevin, the idol head and the premises immediately and not return. It was to go back to where it came from. As he pronounced these words, Kevin—or the spirit in him—squirmed in discomfort. The helpers held onto him.

"No!" Kevin shouted in an altered voice. "I will not go! *You* go and get out of my sight!" There followed a string of obscenities.

"Die!" shrieked Kevin. "Die, all of you!" The spirit lapsed into nonsense in its native tongue.

The deliverance continued with both John and the minister demanding the departure of the spirit, and meeting rigid resistance.

After two hours, Kevin was exhausted, and the energy in the room suddenly broke with a great whooshing sensation. He heaved a great sigh and sank down into the chair, closing his eyes.

"It's gone," John said.

They waited a few minutes, and then Kevin came around. When he opened his eyes, they were clear. He had no recollection of what had happened after he sat down in the chair.

John looked at the idol head. The face and eyes were vacant.

For a long time, they discussed what had taken place, and what still needed to be done. Sometimes spirits fake departing. They lay low and then sneak back in when everyone's guard is down. Kevin and his parents would have to be extremely careful. "No more magic," John said.

"No more," Kevin mumbled.

"All of this stuff has to be removed and cleansed," John said, gesturing around the room.

Kevin nodded.

John gathered up all the occult objects in the room, along with the idol head. On his way out, he pulled Tom and Christine aside. "You will have to be on guard for a very long time," he said. "He can never get involved in anything like this again. Call me if you notice anything, the slightest thing, unusual or wrong."

Back at home, John unloaded the objects and prepared them for cleansing. He always did this outside the house first. He never brought anything not cleansed inside to avoid infecting the home.

John laid the objects out in the yard and treated them with sea salt and holy water. He said his special set of prayers while he dispersed the salt and holy water. He gave particular treatment to the idol head, binding any spirit energy attached to it so that it could not be free to latch onto something else.

After several days, the objects were "clear" and he took them inside and performed the same cleansing. The idol, the objects and books were placed in the Museum of the Paranormal.

John felt that the spirit had indeed been banished, but the minister wanted to make certain. Three more deliverances were performed at the home.

In the months that followed, John heard from Christine several times. Kevin was back to his old self and was doing well in school again. He had another job. But every now and then, Christine would stumble upon more hidden ritual objects while cleaning in his room, which was no longer under lock and key. She did not know if he had forgotten about them, or assumed they were no longer important, but she wanted them out of the house. "Please come and get them while he is in school," she requested of John.

The items were candles, papers and small boards with magical symbols scratched on them, and a few more books. John took them away and cleansed them, adding them to the museum.

Kevin may have gone back to his "old self," but he was permanently changed. A person cannot have this kind of attack from the spirit world without scarring. You are never quite the same again. In the back of your mind is the worry that "it" could come back. The scary thing is, that's true. The victim is "marked" in the spirit world. The spirits always know where you are. Some of them will wait a long time, a lifetime if necessary, for their opportunity to slide back in.

Like recovering from alcohol and drug addiction, recovering from a possession is a lifelong commitment. You have to keep your guard up 24-7. Keep your spiritual house in order, keep your thoughts and emotions on a good level. And stay away from conjuring, even as a game or entertainment.

Kevin is now in his thirties. He still stays in touch with John. He knows he is "marked," and he has stayed clean. He is very lucky.

Sometimes people who come to the museum say the idol makes their skin crawl. They feel it is watching them.

They are probably right. Of all the hundreds of objects in the museum, the idol still has the power to unsettle John.

4

How and Why Objects Become Haunted

The fact that objects can house spirits or energy may seem fantastic, but it's ancient knowledge. Our early ancestors, who cultivated relationships with the spirit world, figured out that just about any object can be turned into a bridge to otherworldly realms.

Many objects have been made specifically to house spirits. Masks are the most common. When masks are made for spiritual and ritual purposes, the mask maker invokes a specific spirit or god energy to inhabit the mask as it is constructed. When worn during ritual, the mask helps the wearer to attune to the resident spirit and, in some cases, be temporarily taken over by it for the duration of the ritual. Tourists do not realize the real purpose of many ethnic masks, and acquire them to decorate their homes or become part of collections. Not every mask that goes home with a tourist has a spirit attached, but plenty do—and we get the calls when mask spirits start frolicking about in their new homes. Some of them are none too happy to find themselves in foreign environments. You'll see what we mean when you read "Spirit in the Mask," one of John's most frightening cases of an occupied tribal mask.

Any object has the potential to acquire spirits and form of energy, however—no rituals required. Daily use and emotional attachments, such as having a fondness for a particular favorite object, can imbue an item with sufficient energy to produce types of haunting phenomena later on.

If everyone picked up on all the energies and spirits clinging and attached to objects, we would be quite distracted all of the time, and probably would be unable to own many things. Some people never have a problem and others are quite vulnerable to even the subtlest of energies. It seems that some people are born with an extra sensitivity, and they have all kinds of paranormal experiences throughout their life. We often find these people at the heart of haunted object cases, and other kinds of haunting and spirit activity. Wherever they go, if "something" is present, it will make itself known. There is even a term for this type of person: "encounter-prone."

For many others, a run-in with a haunted object is a once-in-a-lifetime experience, but one they will never forget.

Here are the types of object hauntings we encounter the most. We'll start with energy residues and work up to problematic entities, and curses.

Imprints and Residues

Wherever we focus our attention, we direct streams of our own energy. Objects we own and handle on a daily basis become "ours" in an energetic sense, for they absorb our unique essence, including our thoughts, emotions, and even memories of events and things that have happened to us. The energy forms imprints and residues that linger long after we no longer have an object, even long after we die.

Some psychics are good at reading objects, a skill called psychometry. By handling an object, they get impressions of previous owners and events that happened to them.

Most of the time, the collections of personal energy in an object are far below the level of awareness of most people. Objects pass through a succession of ownerships all the time without anything amiss. Sometimes, however, objects absorb a great deal of personal energy that has the power to affect others.

Take the case of Abbie, who loved to shop for estate jewelry, and had quite an impressive collection. One day she found a large amethyst ring encircled with seed pearls in a vintage gold setting and fell in love with it. She started wearing it every day. Soon she noticed strange impressions and feelings. She felt a heavy sadness whenever she wore the ring for long periods of time. Then Abbie began having flashes of a woman she did not know. The woman was older, and dressed in period clothing. Abbie felt that somehow she was becoming that woman, or the woman was becoming her, taking over her thoughts and feelings. Her house took on an oppressive air, and she began having difficulty sleeping at night.

When she contacted Rosemary, she said her house had suddenly become haunted by an old woman, but she had no explanation for why. Since hauntings do not suddenly flare up without reason, we had to find the cause. By a process of elimination, the ring was identified as the culprit. Rosemary told Abbie to remove it from the house, and when she did, the oppressive atmosphere and phenomena stopped. She and Abbie paid a visit to the store where Abbie had purchased the ring and asked about its history, explaining they were curious about such a fine old piece. Many second-hand dealers do not know the back story of the things they acquire, but fortunately, the woman who owned the shop did in this case. She said the ring's owner had consigned it and other pieces of her jewelry to raise some needed funds. She had mentioned that it was especially hard to part with the amethyst ring, as it had been her favorite for many years. The shop owner also said that the previous owner had recently lost her husband, and had been going through a great deal of grief.

It was evident that an intensity of emotional energy had gone into the ring over a prolonged period of time, which "rubbed off" on Abbie. Would anyone who acquired the ring have had the same experiences? It's hard to gauge, as we all have different sensitivities to subtle forces. Abbie acknowledged that she had a long personal history of paranormal experiences, so she is likely to pick up on energy residues and even spirit presences more easily than many other persons.

Rosemary gave the ring a good cleansing, which is like removing cob-webby, clingy energy. Abbie, however, decided she did not want to chance a return of the phenomena. The ring went on to a new owner, and at last report, had remained inert.

Imprints and residues can be created by repetitive activities that go on in a specific place. For example, objects used in slaughterhouses are exposed every day to the fear, suffering, and deaths of animals. These residues can cling to objects that are used in that environment. Tools and equipment can become haunted and then leak the negative energy into new environments.

Many people have a fascination with collecting souvenirs from the sites of disasters, horrible accidents, and violent acts of crime and war. They do not realize that these objects have been soaked in negative energy, and they become radiators of ill effects.

Ghosts and Earthbounds

Many ghosts fall into the residues and imprints category. They are energies left behind by the living, and if they are strong enough, can haunt a location. Residual ghosts do repetitive actions: footsteps in the same location; thumps, bangs, and noises; smells; doors that won't stay open or closed; and apparitions. Tuning into a residual ghost is like accessing a video or audio recording in psychic space.

Residual ghosts also can lodge in objects, for the same reasons given above: usually an intense emotional connection fostered by the person who died.

Earthbounds are people who do not make a complete transition to the afterlife, but get caught in a twilight, in-between state that is neither in the physical realm nor in the afterlife. They become like ghosts until they are able to finish their transition. Sometimes, transition requires the help of the living, such as mediums and psychics who work in spirit releasement.

People can become earthbound by choice and by having unfinished business and scores to settle with the living. They can become earthbound by accident, such as in a sudden, violent and tragic death through accident, calamity, suicide, or murder.

Earthbounds may gravitate toward objects that are familiar to them, and become attached to them. They can be persuaded to let go and enter the afterlife, but dealing with them is not easy. We have to establish communication, which is difficult in cases where the earthbounds don't realize they are dead. We have to find out why they are stuck, hear their stories, and then persuade them to move on.

Fairies and Elementals

Fairies

Fairies are found around the world. They are beings who live in the natural world (and sometimes in households), who have supernatural powers, and who have a love or hate relationship with humans. They preceded humans on the planet, but lost out to people, retreating further and further into hills and then into the earth. In modern terms, that's into another dimension.

The Christian church painted fairies as fallen angels, demons, and souls of the unbaptized, but they are beings in their own right, just as we are, with a variety of personalities.

Some of them are quite fond of humans, and some are very helpful. Rosemary has had many encounters with fairies that are friendly. Many fairies, however, don't care much for humans. They are tricksters and pranksters, and they act out when offended.

Fairies are capable of attaching to objects and riding into new environments. At first, they might be mistaken for ghosts or poltergeists. They make disturbances, mess up houses, and move objects around.

Elementals

We don't see elemental hauntings often. Elementals are beings tied to the forces of nature: air, earth, water and fire. They are sometimes classed with fairies, but they are distinctly different. They have different names, according to their elements. Water elementals are sometimes called undines and nymphs; earth elementals are called gnomes and pigmies; fire elementals are called salamanders; and air elementals are called sylphs.

Paracelsus, the great sixteenth-century Swiss alchemist and philosopher, wrote a great deal on elementals. He said they are neither spirits nor related to humans, but occupy both the physical and spiritual worlds. They can take human form if they desire.

Elementals rarely seek out interaction with human beings. According to Paracelsus, the undines, nymphs, and sylphs are the most likely to interact with people. Elementals can be summoned in magic, and under certain circumstances they might find their way to objects and attach to them.

Demons, Spirits and Beings

There are a wide variety of intelligent entities that can lodge in objects and cause hauntings.

Demons and spirits

In 1Western culture, the word "demon" has become synonymous with evil beings that serve Satan and cause horrible problems, including possession. The word is so loaded that we often prefer to call most of these beings "spirits," because their trouble-making falls short of Hollywood-style horror films. True, the bad guys do exist, and we deal with them in plenty of heavy-duty cases. In many cases of haunted objects, however, the demonic culprits are low-level mischief makers. They are still irritating and capable of wreaking havoc in people's lives, but they fall short of *The Exorcist*.

Mischief-making is exactly how our ancestors viewed much of the demonic realm. The spirit realm teems with all kinds of spirits that are in general labeled "demons" who interfere in the affairs of people. In the ancient view, demons were not necessarily all bad, but ranged from good to neutral to evil. The word "demon" is derived from the Greek term *daimon*. The *daimones* were both good and evil, and even included deified heroes. You may have heard of Socrates' famous *daimones*—the philosopher said he had a good one that whispered in one ear giving him advice, and a bad one that whispered in the other ear, creating a constant tug-of-war between taking right or wrong actions.

The ancient Babylonians, Assyrians, and other early Middle Eastern cultures believed in a supernatural realm full of demons, whose main attack on humans was illness. The attacking demons invaded bodies, and had to be cast out.

Judaic demonologies were influenced by Middle Eastern beliefs. In Talmudic tradition, demons are ever-present enemies posing constant dangers to humanity. They were created by God on the first Sabbath eve at twilight. Dusk fell before God finished them, and thus they have no bodies. According to another story, demons were spawned by Lilith, the spurned first wife of Adam.

In the Christian view, demons are the soldiers of Satan, created from the ranks of fallen angels who followed Lucifer when he was cast out of heaven by God because of his pride (Isaiah 14:12). Demons are always evil and are dedicated to tormenting people and leading them astray so that their souls are condemned.

Theologians organized demons into hierarchies with legions of demonic soldiers working for chains of higher-ranking demons. Occultists created magical rituals for summoning demons in the hopes of commanding them to carry out tasks—always a risky procedure that could easily backfire on the summoner.

No matter what their disposition and origin, demons have always been regarded as troublesome and responsible for all the bad things that happen to people, including disease, accidents, poor health, bad luck, ruined relationships, and soul loss. Ancient peoples identified and named many types of demons according to their characteristics as tricksters, sexual predators, soul stealers, and so on.

In the modern West, demons are regarded as evil heavy hitters that infest, oppress, and possess. So, to avoid confusion, we use "demon" as a term to describe those satanic beings, and "spirit" to describe lesser pesky beings that cause some of the haunting problems we find associated with objects.

Demons and spirits are not dull or stupid, but intelligent and crafty entities. They know how to hide and wait for opportunities, so no wonder that certain objects become the ideal vehicles for them.

How do demons and spirits become attached to objects?

One way is through binding. A ritual is performed to summon a demon or spirit and bind it to an object (often a piece of jewelry or a small object) that then serves as its home. The demon is released ritually whenever it is sent out on an errand or asked for information, and then ordered back to its home when everything is done. Traditionally, demons were bound and used for divination of the future, finding treasure, procuring love, and providing information.

Most people today do not perform this kind of ritual magic, but it is possible to pick up the stray "spirit house" object for sale in flea markets, estate and antique shops, antique auctions, yard sales and so on. No one knows the object has a "rider" until it goes to the right environment where the occupying entity can get loose and start acting out.

Another way that demons and spirits become attached to objects is through an energetic link of imprints and residues. For example, a person has an interest in the spirit realms and does a lot of reading, study, and other pursuits, but does not engage in ritual magic. This interest attracts a variety of beings to that person, and these beings then "hang out" a lot. They may not ever obviously bother or influence the original person, but if circumstances are right, they may be able to latch on to favorite personal possessions, and, as the objects pass ownership, get loose. We have had cases in which we have been able to trace the ownership history of objects to people who have had an active interest in the occult, and perhaps even experimented with rituals and spell casting. Such activities are never innocent and without consequence. Even if rituals are done for a good purpose, they create doorways for spirits who leave residues that go unnoticed—and uncorrected—by novices.

One of the most famous—or perhaps we should say infamous— objects of energetic attachments is the Ouija, as well as similar "talking board" divination devices. As we point out in John's *Shadows of the Dark* and in *Ouija Gone Wild* by Rosemary and Rick Fisher, the Ouija is often misused, causing supernatural problems for users. Low-level trickster and malicious entities sometimes attach to the board, as well as to the people working the board.

The board scenarios are all similar. A person or group tries out a board for fun and gets responses to questions. Sometimes the answering entity is jolly and amusing, and provides accurate information. The users become so fascinated that they spend more and more time working the board, and become increasingly open to what now is a dominant communicator. That entity then suddenly turns dark and nasty, making threats against the users. The users are plagued with unpleasant phenomena and feel out of control. Before they realize it, they are taken over by the entity that has invaded their personal space.

In the worst cases, stopping board use and even getting rid of the board does not stop the activity, for the spirits are able to literally jump ship and attach to people and the environment. The remedies then have to go far beyond neutralizing the boards, but also involve house exorcisms and spirit detachments.

We've had our share of haunted Ouija boards, including two that were featured in *Haunted Collector*, in which John called in Rosemary for consultation. In most cases, households erupted in frightening paranormal phenomena and activity. Victims were physically attacked, suffered health issues, and were plagued with all sorts of paranormal manifestations.

Imps

Imps are low-level demons that can be magically bound to an object such as a bottle or ring for the purpose of service. "Imp" is an old term that was used frequently during the Inquisition in the trials of accused witches, who supposedly kept and used imps to carry out tasks and even dark deeds. The imps were said to shape-shift into different forms, usually animal. The witch fed them with his or her own blood.

Many of those charges against accused witches were trumped up, but there is a basis to the imp. Demon and spirits do shape-shift, and there are many accounts throughout history of blood being used to attract and reward certain kinds of spirits.

Today the term "imp" isn't used much, but when it is, it usually applies to a mischievous or trickster type of entity, one who likes to play pranks, make a lot of noise, and cause disruption.

Familiars

In earlier times, "familiar" was a term for imp and also demon, applying especially to an entity that had a close relationship with a human. Familiars are a type of servant demon attached to a person. The familiar performs tasks, provides guardianship, and gives advice, information and instruction. The term "familiar" comes from the Latin term *familiaris*, meaning "of a household or domestic."

Like imps and many demons, familiars can be either good or evil in nature, and they vary significantly in intelligence and power. They shape-shift into many forms, including animal and human. They can be bound to objects with instructions to carry out attacks and curses.

Djinn

Most of the world has been familiar with Djinn for centuries, but we in the West are still in the dark about these powerful beings. Djinn, whose Arabic name means "the Hidden Ones," were here on the planet first, and, like the fairies, lost out to human domination. They were said to be made of the wind, or of "smokeless fire," that is, with no definite physical form. The French corrupted their name to "genie," and that's how most of us know them today—as the genie in the bottle who grants wishes. We only know them through the old Arabian Nights folk tales, such as Aladdin and his magical lamp.

According to lore, the animosity between Djinn and humans goes back to the creation of Adam. In the account told in the Qur'an, the Djinn refused to bow to Adam on God's orders, on the grounds that the newly created human was inferior to them. For that they were banished, but were given until Judgment Day to make their case that humans are weak and inferior.

Djinn are not fantasy but are real beings. They are superb shape-shifters, and quite crafty. Throughout the ages, they have been blamed, like demons, for all bad things that happen to people. They are capable of masquerading as other beings and even humans. They can act like ghosts, poltergeists, demons, fairies, and elementals. A single Djinn can create a variety of manifestations, so that victims think they are under assault by all sorts of supernatural beings.

Djinn usually become involved with humans when it suits their purpose, and so they attach to a person or family, usually for the purposes of tormenting, or vampirizing their life force. Or, they become angered when their turf is invaded, for many of them have strong attachments to land. They also become vengeful when they are harmed, wronged, and slighted, and when they are summoned for favors and then not paid.

Djinn can be bound to objects, or summoned by sorcerers to impart their energy into objects. This takes a great deal of skill as well as a hefty price that is paid to the Djinn, who will collect, whether from the sorcerer or clients, or even his descendants. The internet is full of sales pitches for rings, pendants, and bottles that supposedly contain Djinn who can be commanded to serve the owners. Don't fall for it. Most likely, you will get something that is magically empty. If you get an object that has been empowered, you will find the tables turned on you in short order. Djinn trapped in vessels are not in a good mood when they are released.

Few people understand the difficulties of trying to control Djinn or any kind of entity. We frequently hear from cocky people who think dealing with the spirit world is child's play. It is not, and powerful beings and spirits will gain the upper hand before you know they've done it. At that point, you'll be calling us for help to get out of a mess.

Check out our story "Be Careful What You Wish For," about an old oil lamp that now resides in John's museum. For other eye-openers, visit Rosemary's website on the Djinn, www.djinnuniverse.com.

Curses

Many of our cases involve objects that have been cursed. A cursed object carries a negative energy that spills out into an environment and wreaks havoc upon the victims in the form of bad luck, ruined relationships, ill health, accidents, nightmares, and unpleasant phenomena. Some cursed objects are bound with spirits or demonic beings who carry out attacks.

Curses caused by tragedy

Objects can be cursed by bad circumstances, similar to the residual effects we discussed earlier. In these cases, however, the fallout is much more severe, with serious and even life-threatening consequences. The objects are more than haunted—they are truly cursed.

For example, stolen items, especially from sacred places, might become cursed because of the violation of the crime. Objects from desecrated graves can become cursed, as can the possessions and even body parts of people who have died violently, tragically, and unhappily.

The famous "screaming skulls" of England are said to be haunted by restless spirits of the dead who died at the hands of soldiers, kings, robbers, and murderers. In some cases, their final deathbed wishes were ignored. Folklore holds that when the wishes of the dying are not respected, their spirits will remained agitated and restless.

The screaming skulls became souvenir objects of morbid interest and were kept on display in houses. The skulls reportedly made screaming noises at night, moving around and creating poltergeist disturbances such as bangs and crashes. Some brought their owners bad luck. Most of the stories behind the skulls are more legend than fact, but the black cloud of ill fortune clings to them just the same.

A famous curse story concerns the "Little Bastard," the car driven by actor James Dean when he had his fatal, horrific crash in September 1955. Dean was a speed freak and often drove his sports cars and motorcycles at breakneck speeds just for the thrill of it. He often joked that he was destined to die in a speeding car.

In 1955, Dean was filming *Giant* in Texas. After he returned to Los Angeles, he bought a new silver-gray Porsche Spider with the intention of driving in an upcoming competition race in Salinas. He persuaded a

Porsche mechanic, Rolf Wuetherich, to come along with him. Some of Dean's friends had bad feelings about the car and tried unsuccessfully to persuade him to get rid of it. Perhaps they were getting precognitive feelings about his impending death.

En route to the race at Salinas, Dean crashed head-on into a car driven by a college student, and was killed instantly. Wuetherich was thrown free and suffered moderate injuries, and the college student, Donald Turnupseed, suffered only minor cuts.

The Porsche, badly mangled, was sold and salvaged for parts. Immediately stories arose that horrible things happened to people who handled or used the parts. The mangled car fell on a mechanic when it was unloaded at a garage and broke one of his legs. Souvenir hunters who tried to steal parts off the wreckage were seriously injured. People who used Little Bastard parts and tires in their own vehicle suffered serious crashes and accidents. Spooked, the owner of the wrecked car stopped selling parts and decided to put the vehicle on display—but wherever the car went, mishap, misfortune, and injury occurred. In 1960, the Little Bastard mysteriously disappeared.

Another bizarre curse story concerns a doomed jet airliner, Eastern Airlines Flight 401, which crashed in the Florida Everglades on December 19, 1972 as it was attempting to land in Miami. Everyone aboard the L-1011 jumbo jet—more than 100 persons—perished. Eastern Airlines salvaged parts from the wreckage and used them in other jets, including planes leased to other airlines. Wherever the cursed parts went, the uniformed ghosts of some of the ill-fated crew were seen. Apparently no mishaps occurred, unlike the Little Bastard curse, but the ghosts aboard planes were nonetheless quite unnerving.

Tragic, violent death releases powerful energy that sears itself into objects. Not every object associated with tragic death becomes haunted and cursed, but many do. Tragedy also holds a powerful attraction to the living. Souvenir hunters wanting a piece of gruesome history will scavenge whatever they can, and sometimes sell these items as collectibles for high prices. Folklore holds that profiting on the tragedy of others will bring bad luck. Judging from the cases we get, we can certainly say that's true.

A tragic or violent death does not have to be high-profile to create a problem. The residual fallout of many of life's problems and tragedies gets passed on all the time in curios, estate pieces, and other secondhand items.

Some of our stories in this book are about objects cursed this way, such as "The Scornful Military Jacket," about a vintage jacket that held the energy of war and combat.

Curses caused by ill will

Far deadlier than tragedy curses are deliberate curses, planned by vengeful and spiteful people to harm specific individuals. We see a lot of those cases, too. There is no shortage of anger and hate channeled into vicious attacks. The perpetrators don't use guns, knives, or poison. Their weapons are far more insidious: innocent-looking objects usually given as gifts, but secretly carrying curses intended to bring about another person's downfall.

Cursed objects are seldom recognized by the victims, who may even be charmed by the gift itself. The objects are Trojan horses. Once inside the gates—inside the victim's house and accepted into his or her possession—they unleash the curse, and sometimes even a spirit or familiar to carry it out.

The most common reasons why people send cursed objects to others have remained the same throughout history: love, money, and power. Jilted lovers, unrequited lovers, thwarted lovers, and jealous lovers have resorted to magical curses to get rid of rivals and to take revenge on the one who spurned them. People send curses over financial deals gone sour, bad debts, cons and swindles, refusals for loans, and in anger over inheritances. Curses also are sent against rivals for power of all sorts. Name your profession, sport, or politics, there are sore losers everywhere, and some of them don't want to forgive and forget. In fact, just about any slight or grievance that makes a person feel deeply wronged can become grist for a curse.

How can objects be deliberately cursed so that they become paranormal time bombs?

The simplest way is through an act of ill wishing, or thinking venomous thoughts about someone. We all have episodes where we get mad at others and wish them ill rather than well, and most of the time, that energy is not organized and goes spinning off into etheric space. If a great deal of time and energy is focused on negative thoughts directed at a person, the energy transforms into a thoughtform and takes on a real power and force. Holding an object while focusing that energy puts the intention into the object, and voila—you have a cursed object.

There are formal ritual ways to accomplish the same thing: spells and incantations, and the summoning of dark beings that will carry out specific attacks. Many people bent on cursing will seek out a magically empowered person, such as a sorcerer, to "throw" the curse.

Cursing has a long and quite checkered history. Today we consider cursing unethical and even a violation of spiritual laws, but our ancestors felt much differently: cursing was a way of doing business. The ancient Egyptians did a lot of cursing, judging from surviving papyri texts. The Greeks and Romans followed suit. Curses were written on tablets, strips of lead, and bits of parchment. They cited the victim and the grievance and petitioned spirits or else the dead, who were regarded as wielding great power from beyond the grave, to take a desired action. Such written curses were often fixed with nails and thrown into wells, springs or rivers where the spirits were believed to reside. If the dead were invoked, the curses were buried near a fresh tomb, a battlefield, or an execution site, all places of power.

The Romans excelled at cursing, and leveled them against any rival in any sphere of life. Cursing was just one of the ways a person sought to gain advantage over another. Take, for example, this dire curse against a charioteer competing in a race:

> I conjure you, daemon, whoever you may be, to torture and kill, from this hour, this day, this moment, the horses of the Green and the White teams; kill and smash the charioteers Clarus, Felix, Primulus, Romanus; do not leave breath in them…

On into history cursing continued in many forms. Blasting was a curse of ruination, such as to cause the withering of crops and the deaths of farm animals—the sources of people's livelihoods and ability to survive.

Mutilating and sticking pins in a substitute for the victim, such as a doll or poppet, is an old form of cursing that carries even more power when the poppet is delivered to the victim, whose fear aids the curse. Poppets are still used in modern cursing, along with pictures, portraits, and photographs. The substitute item establishes a sympathetic connection to the victim that enables the energy of the curse to travel, like electricity along a wire, to its intended target. The sympathetic connection can be strengthened by the addition of the victim's hair, nail clippings, or bits of clothing.

We've seen all kinds of poppets: store-bought dolls that are altered, and cloth dolls made from scratch by the perpetrators of the curses. In such cases, the curse is broken by severing the sympathetic link and neutralizing the objects neutralized.

On a trip to Monterrey, Mexico, Rosemary went out on an investigation with a leading paranormal group. One of their primary activities was going into cemeteries at night to find cursed objects buried at gravesites and deactivate them. The people who threw the curses were calling upon the dead to lend a supernatural hand. The curse items consisted of a variety of things, and included a payment to the dead for their help, such as cigarettes, alcohol, fruits, and meat. Poppets, photographs, personal effects, and written curses were sometimes buried with the offerings, along with stones and herbs to add energy to the curse. Most of these curses, Rosemary was told, involved thwarted love, and the cursing was a common tactic. The investigators knew where to find the curse bags and objects because of information provided in their casework, and they also used psychics to find unknown ones. After unearthing the objects, an exorcist ritually deactivated them to break the curses.

In our line of work, we see many cases involving thwarted love. The deadliest curse objects are not buried in graves but are gifts and ordinary items that most people would never suspect to be infused with harmful energy. Examples of love gone wrong curses are told in "Jewelry Cursed By A Jilted Witch," about a jealous woman who used infected jewelry to attack a man with a curse on his wedding night, and "The Squishy Faces," a creepy tale about an ex-lover with a grudge. "The Squishy Faces" is especially odd because the cursed items were bookends that were not at all attractive, but the victim felt obliged to accept and keep them because they were handmade by his ex-lover.

Fortunately, most people find other ways to settle scores and get over disputes, but even a few people determined to curse can still create major havoc. What the cursers do not realize, however, is that they become the real victims. They may succeed in making their targets suffer, but ultimately they will pay a similar price, for curses have a nasty way of boomeranging back on the senders. It might not happen immediately, but a reckoning always comes.

Thoughtforms

A thoughtform is a nonphysical entity literally created by thought. They are sometimes called "artificial elementals." Some thoughtforms are created spontaneously by intense emotional energy and thought. Other thoughtforms can be created deliberately through spells and rituals. The thoughtforms can be instructed and tasked in ways similar to spirits, such as to guard and protect—or to attach to an object and attack whoever receives the object. They can take whatever form has been programmed into them. They may look like humans, human ghosts, monstrous specters, or animals.

The lifespan and endurance of a thoughtform depends on the nature and intensity of the thought that created it; the programming that is put into it; and the skill of the person creating the thoughtform. Most thoughtforms run down like batteries and dissipate, unless they are continually fed and energized by their maker. When created, thoughtforms usually are charged with a limited lifespan. If they are improperly created, they can amass enough energy to gain a certain level of intelligence and independence, and the ability to act on their own. Out-of-control thoughtforms are as dangerous as malevolent spirits.

A Complex World

This has been a short tour of the spirit realm and the reasons why objects can become haunted. Our physical world is quite complex: our reality is interwoven with the spirit realm. We live side by side with all kinds of invisible residents who share the planet with us. The haunting of objects goes beyond supernatural thriller stories. The cases we describe here in this book have a great deal to teach us about our unseen neighbors.

5

The Deathbed

The scream tore through the house. Brad, comfortably slouched down in the sofa with a bowl of chips and a soda, was jolted so much that the chips nearly flew out of the bowl. He yanked his feet off of the new coffee table as his girlfriend, Laura, came racing down the hall and exploded into the living room. Her face was pasty white.

"That's *it!*" Laura shrieked, gesturing wildly with her arms. "I can't stay in this house any longer!" She put her head down into her hands and started sobbing.

Brad wiped his hands on his jeans and stood up. He went to Laura and hugged her, smoothing down her long blonde hair. "Calm down," he said. "What happened? Was it that *thing* again?"

Still sobbing, Laura nodded. "That black shadow thing! I see it every time I'm in the hall now. Brad, it *followed* me out of the bedroom! I thought something was behind me and I turned around and looked—" She broke down again. "It acted like it was going to grab me! And look! I've been scratched—again!" She held out her right arm. Her inside forearm had a long, red scratch, as though a sharp point had raked the surface of the skin.

Brad tried to comfort her while keeping an eye on the football game at the same time. "It's okay, baby, it's okay. I know it's creepy when you think you see that thing."

Laura pulled herself back and stared at Brad with a horrified look. "I've told you, this is not my imagination. I'm not making it up. I see it and it scares me to death! And how do you explain all these scratches—that we *both* get? Do we make those up, too?"

Brad shrugged. "Like I told you, I think we've been careless and didn't realize we got scratched."

"Oh, that's ridiculous!" Laura glared at him. "You don't care what happens to me, do you?"

"That's not true—"

Laura stabbed a finger at the coffee table. "Ever since we brought that—that *deathbed* into the house, all sorts of horrible things go on. I asked you to get rid of it. Nobody wants it and now we know why. Well, I've had it! It's me or it. I'm leaving and I'm not coming back until it's out of here!"

Laura spun on her heels and marched down the hall to their master bedroom. Brad heard drawers being jerked opened and clothes flung about.

No amount of persuasion made a dent on Laura as she threw clothes and belongings into two suitcases. By the time she was done packing, the two of them were screaming at each other in a heated argument. They had been having quite of few of those lately, ever since a certain piece of furniture arrived.

A piece of furniture from hell.

Despite Brad's confidence that Laura would come to her senses, she refused to return to the house. A cold loneliness settled into the place in her absence. Brad was not alone, however—the dark, shadowy form glided around the house, bolder than ever. Usually Brad saw it in the hallway, but it made increasing appearances elsewhere in the house.

"Get the f— out of here!" Brad shouted at it whenever he saw it. Previously the globby shadow evaporated or disappeared around a corner when Brad yelled at it, but now it stood its ground.

There were other upsetting phenomena as well. Raps and bangs on the walls at night. A pervasive atmosphere of foreboding. Nightmares almost every night. Brad, who was rarely sick, felt erosion on his health.

He made a decision.

John had just gotten home from a weekend-long paranormal conference and was looking forward to chilling out for the evening. As usual after an absence, the voicemails for both his home phone and cell phone were overflowing. He skipped through the ones that could wait. One of the messages riveted his attention.

"Mr. Zaffis," began a male voice. "I have something for you. It's a deathbed and I think it's possessed. I was going to take it outside and burn it or chop it up, but someone gave me your number. Soooo…" the voice trailed off and then picked up. "Here's my number."

A deathbed! What did the man mean? John wasted no time returning the call. This wasn't the first time he'd heard people threaten to destroy objects they believed were "possessed." There were a few cases when he didn't arrive in time, only to find out the offending item had been tossed into an incinerator or taken to a landfill, or even chucked into the ocean. An object as large as a bed could not be disposed of easily—but it could be turned into kindling. When people become upset, they take drastic action.

Brad sounded matter-of-fact on the phone as he recounted recent events leading up to the departure of his girlfriend. He described the deathbed. "It's a big wooden slab with short legs, with this headrest on one end. They said it was used for dead people. They told me it came from somewhere in Africa."

"Who are 'they'?" John asked.

"The people I got it from at work," Brad said. "They wanted to get rid of it because of the things that started happening to them."

"Okay, and what did you do with it? You're not running a funeral home are you?" John said jokingly.

Brad sighed. "We thought it would make a cool coffee table."

A deathbed turned into a coffee table? John had seen many coffins turned into coffee tables, but a deathbed was a new twist. What kind of trouble had these people gotten themselves into?

After getting more information, John told Brad he would be there as soon as possible. He wasn't certain how he was going to get the bed home, but he would at least get there, rescue it, and sort out the return logistics. He threw some clothes into a small bag.

Thirteen hours and a gallon or two of coffee later, John pulled into Brad's driveway after a tiring marathon drive. Along the way, he had had several phone checks with Brad to make certain everything was still on track.

Brad looked to be in his early thirties. He was a nice looking man with straight dark hair. His brown eyes looked tired, like those of a person under stress. "Hey man," he greeted John, as though he were an old friend. He wasted no time leading John to the deathbed. Another young man, a friend of Brad's, was in the living room. Brad introduced him only as "Robbie." John had the impression that Robbie had come to lend Brad some moral support.

The deathbed was an impressive piece: a thick, wide, dark-stained slab of wood about eight feet long, with a saddle on one end. It was hand-hewn. An air of sadness clung to it. John pictured a body laid at rest on it.

Brad told him how he had acquired this unusual piece of furniture. An executive where he worked was a veteran international traveler, and a collector of exotic items. He and his wife took a trip to Africa and returned with masks, tribal ritual objects, art, and other items. One of his acquisitions was the deathbed, which he arranged to have shipped to his home. Brad was not certain exactly where it had been purchased. The story behind it was that it had been used for the viewing of bodies before they were cremated.

The executive's wife was opposed to the deathbed's purchase from the beginning, Brad said. She did not want it in the house, but her husband prevailed. Soon after the deathbed arrived, the couple began experiencing peculiar phenomena in the house: a dark, shadowy form and disturbing noises in the night. The wife fell ill and could not get better. She begged her husband to get rid of the deathbed, but he rejected her conviction that it was related to her ill health, or to any of the disturbances that plagued the house. Her health deteriorated.

At some point, according to Brad, the husband became spooked about the bed and decided he wanted it out of the house immediately. He was preparing to have it carted away when an employee at work offered to take it off of his hands. This man did not believe in the paranormal or supernatural, and thought the deathbed was a unique curiosity and prize. He did not have to pay for it—the executive was relieved to get rid of it.

The deathbed went to its new home, where it was put on display. Within two weeks, however, the same phenomena infected the second owner's home. His wife, too, thought the deathbed brought an unpleasant presence into the house. She persuaded her husband to get rid it.

Brad heard the stories at work and was intrigued. He did not believe that an object had any special supernatural power. In fact, the stories added to the deathbed's allure. How many people would ever own such an object? He'd heard that the executive had paid a great deal of money for it. Now his co-worker, the new owner, wanted to dump it for free. He told Laura about it, but she was reluctant to take it. He convinced her that everyone else had let their imaginations run wild.

The second owner of the deathbed tried to warn him off. "Don't take it, don't even go near it, man," the co-worker said. "It's got a real bad vibe. It ought to be destroyed."

The warning made Brad want to own the bed more than ever. There's nothing like the thrill of danger. He persuaded the man to let him take the bed.

The warning proved to be right. Ever since the deathbed had come into Brad's house, unsettling things had occurred. The appearances of the shadow figure were especially unnerving to Laura. Brad still believed that the phenomena were the result of over-worked imagination, however, and he shrugged everything off.

Now, Brad admitted to John that secretly he liked the commotion—he bragged about it at work. The deathbed had lots of "dine out" cachet. Laura's departure, however, changed everything.

John knew that in some cultures bodies awaiting cremation were laid out on plank-like viewing beds or platforms, and that sometimes everything, including the plank, went into the fire. This piece was far too substantial for such a single use, unless it had been made for a very important and wealthy person. Perhaps it had served instead as a viewing bed for many bodies prior to their final disposition, whether it be burial or cremation.

Brad was unable to tell John any more details about its history.

"Would it be possible to talk to the previous owners, especially the man who brought this back from Africa?" John asked.

Brad shook his head. "Please don't. That would not be a good idea. Nobody wants to talk about it." He refused to say more. Apparently everyone who had come into contact with the deathbed was too spooked to discuss it.

John did a walk-through of the house. He sensed a presence attached to the deathbed. In cases where a human earthbound spirit might be attached to the object, John always tried a few tactics to see if energy shifted, and if a personality could—and would—communicate and give a name. Then he would take steps to help it cross over into the afterlife. Whatever was attached to the deathbed, however, was not making itself known right away.

John said prayers over the deathbed and sprinkled it with holy water and sea salt. He waited to see the reaction. No information came from the attached spirit, but the atmosphere in the house became more highly charged. Brad and Robbie started arguing about the deathbed. John decided not to pursue anything else with the spirit until he got the deathbed safely home.

The bed was heavy, like a slab of concrete. It took all three men to lift it and get it strapped to the roof of John's car. It looked comical, like an oversized surfboard. John hoped it would survive the long trip home.

"Will this end what's been going on?" said Brad, a worried look on his face. "It's not going to come back on me, is it?"

John replied that removing the deathbed would probably end the paranormal activity, but there was no guarantee that more measures would not have to be taken. "Call me if you have more problems," he said. Brad nodded.

John glanced in the side view mirror as he pulled out of the driveway. Brad looked profoundly relieved.

John took a more leisurely drive back, and stopped for the night at a motel. As he entered the lobby to register, the desk clerk, an African American, looked over his shoulder out the window to where John's car was parked. The man shook his head. "Bad," he said in a heavily accented voice. "Bad mojo, bad mojo, bad mojo." He was considerably agitated.

John wanted to question him about the deathbed to glean more information, but feared spooking the man altogether.

The next morning, John found a small cluster of motel employees standing a good distance from his car. They were focused on the deathbed, gesturing at it and talking in low voices.

This time, John decided to speak up. He approached them and said, "Can any of you tell me anything about this?" He pointed to the deathbed.

The employees at once looked frightened. Without a word, they all dispersed.

Whatever the bed represented, others seemed to know exactly all about it.

Back home, John maneuvered the deathbed onto his front lawn. It was a sunny, bright day, and he wanted to expose it to the cleansing solar rays. He sprinkled it again with holy water and sea salt, said prayers over it, and infused it with positive energy. While it sat outside, John sorted out space for the massive object. The Museum of the Paranormal was overflowing with haunted objects.

John rearranged the small meeting room next to his office and placed the deathbed along one wall. It conveniently served as display space for other items. The deathbed was quiet, but it exuded a palpable energy field that visitors found disturbing. Whatever was attached to it would not communicate.

Rosemary could not wait to examine the deathbed. "Weird vibe," she said when she saw it. "That's the only way I can describe it."

"Everyone who sees it says that," said John. "It affects everybody."

Finding similar deathbeds from Africa proved to be difficult. Perhaps it was not native to any African country, but had been imported by a Hindu family. Research revealed that according to prevailing Hindu custom, a body is laid out for viewing in a coffin, and both body and coffin go into a crematorium. In the case of funeral processions of well-known people, the body is placed on a pallet that is carried through the streets.

John consulted a variety of sources and was told different things about the deathbed's purpose. He was told it had been made for a single purpose, to hold a body and be cremated along with it. He also was told that it probably had been placed in a hut for funeral services and viewing, and had held many bodies.

Rosemary contacted one of her sources in northern Africa who was knowledgeable about burial customs, and was told that cremation practices among various tribes are rare. If the bed had been used as part of cremation, then it probably was linked to Hindus living in Africa, perhaps in Kenya.

As for traditional African practices, a body might be kept for viewing for a few days and then buried. Great care is taken to inter a body in the deceased person's ancestral home, lest his spirit be angry and return to harass the living. In some areas, there are customs of spilling gasoline on the coffin after it is placed in its hole in the ground and setting it afire, in order to drive the spirit away. Every tribe has its elaborate rules governing the proper burial of the dead.

"Anything like that holding bed would be seen as accursed in African culture," the source said. "They would think that your friend would be nuts for bringing something like that into their home. That would definitely bring the spirit back and it would begin lashing out in the exact manner you have described—sickness, bad luck, disasters, et cetera. The dead are feared and are known to cause misfortunes to the living when they are either forgotten or upset about something.

"That bed would definitely be a magnet to whatever spirit lay on it. It also would open the door to the ancestral spirits of that family line to exact revenge on the person that they are upset with, such as the one who took the bed. With Africans, it's never one spirit, but a host of them—generations."

There was another possibility, the source said. The owner of the deathbed in Africa might have been plagued by an unhappy spirit attached to it and might have sold the bed in order to pass the problem on to someone else, such as an unsuspecting tourist. "That is how many Africans deal with supernatural issues," the source said. "They pass them on to another person. Bringing such an article back to your house would definitely invite misfortune.

"That is some bad energy on that table," he went on. "Let it be locked up in the museum where it belongs. When you see objects being quickly gotten rid of in Africa, there is some major bad energy on them. Chances are the original owner went for consultation with a witch doctor about his problems and the best advice was to pass the darkness onto someone else, thus removing it from his family."

Getting rid of a curse by passing it on is a widespread practice around the world, so that scenario made sense. Perhaps the spirit of a dead person who had been placed on the bed in Africa, had attached to it. When the bed passed into private ownership, the spirit lashed out at the owner, who then solved his problem by selling the bed. Once in America, the spirit became especially upset and angry at being transported to a foreign location, away from all its ancestral connections.

Another possibility occurred to John. Perhaps the attached spirit was actually a guardian of the deathbed. It, too, was unhappy to be removed from its rightful homeland.

There was yet another possibility. The shadowy form and the haunting phenomena may have been thoughtform energies that collected from many corpses, and gained enough energy to take on a supernatural life.

Whatever the explanation, the bed now rests quietly in John's museum, one of the most unusual objects he has encountered in his career.

There were no more calls from Brad, indicating that all was now quiet in his home as well.

The deathbed case goes beyond a spirit attachment to an object, however. Any objects that have been used for sacred purpose—and taking care of the dead is most sacred—should never be turned into common household furnishings or amusement pieces. The dead and their guardians do not take kindly to disrespect.

The case reminded John of an earlier case he had had with a wealthy family. They, too, were collectors of the exotic, but on a much bigger scale. On a trip to Europe, the husband and wife fell in love with a quaint, small eighteenth-century Catholic chapel. The chapel and its furnishings were exquisite, hand-made of the finest materials by skilled craftsmen and artists. For no small price—some two to three million dollars—they purchased the entire chapel, had it carefully dismantled, and then shipped to America. They then had it reconstructed within their own home.

Unfriendly paranormal activity was immediate, and escalated to the point where no one in the family could even enter the chapel room without feeling attacked. John was contacted. He began a long process of elimination to identify the object responsible, but when all were eliminated, he had to conclude that it was the chapel itself.

John informed them that something was offended by their removal of a sacred structure from its native place. Furthermore, he said, "Those are spiritual things that are never meant to be brought into a home."

The husband seemed puzzled by this. "You're kidding," he said. "To me they are objects of great beauty."

"They are," replied John, "but they are still not meant to be used in the home."

"We can't ship it back," the husband fumed. "You have no idea how much money is already sunk into this."

John's hands were tied. He was certain the family was not likely to have any relief of the paranormal activity as long as the chapel remained in their home.

The family consulted local Catholic authorities. A bishop became involved, and agreed that they had committed a serious mistake and should remove the chapel from their home. The family arranged for clergy to come and do blessings—which John anticipated would have little lasting impact, considering the fundamental nature of the problem.

At last the family decided to dismantle the chapel and have it removed. Instead of sending it back to its native land, however, they decided that all the pieces would be auctioned off. The husband reminded John again of the "huge investment" he had in the chapel, and he had to recover as much as possible. That was the last John heard of the matter.

From our perspective, it was a poor solution. The income from the auctioned pieces would be "tainted money," and had the potential to lead to other problems. And, the auctioned pieces were going to be passed on to unsuspecting buyers. Would some of them experience the same phenomena? We'll probably never know.

People do acquire religious and sacred objects all the time for display in their homes, yet not everyone experiences problems. Variables depend on the objects themselves and how they are regarded, displayed, and used. Even with the right attitude towards such an object, an attachment problem might occur. Every case has to be evaluated on its own.

Ordinary objects that are surgically removed from places and "repurposed" also can become associated with haunting activity. One of Rosemary's cases involved a famous castle-like home in America that contained items from abroad that had captured the fancy of its wealthy builder, among them a sixteenth-century oak and iron double door, an entire staircase, and beautiful stained glass windows. The house was quite haunted. The massive oak and iron door was a particular focal point. Witnesses often saw men and women in period clothing pass through it.

Footsteps were heard and presences were felt on the staircase, among many other kinds of activity.

The presences of the old, the antique, and the ancient are around us all the time. We live among the remnants and reminders of the past, and often incorporate them into our lives. Sometimes the Unseen World rejoices that something once loved is loved and appreciated again—and sometimes the Unseen World objects

6

Possessed Mirrors

Mirror, mirror, on the wall... who is the most haunted of them all?
Me, me, look into me... I have a big surprise... You will see!

Ray knew "they" were hiding in the mirror. And it terrified him.

Ever since the mirror had been installed in their dining room, things were not right. Things were not right in the house and they were not right deep inside of him. He was isolated in his fear, for his wife dismissed the notion that anything was wrong. Even in the face of unexplained activity.

"I'm telling you, there are these black shapes that go into the mirror," Ray insisted to his wife, Aleen, as she hand dried dishes after their dinner. "I *see* them. When I do, they go into the mirror. Like that!" He snapped his fingers.

Aleen gave her husband a quizzical look. He was a big dude, a biker, and—until now—fearless. She had never heard him talk about ghosts or shadow beings, or weird mirrors. She wondered what had gotten into him lately.

"And *I* keep telling *you*, I don't see anything," Aleen said. "Have you been watching those ghost shows on TV?"

"*No*," said Ray. "But I think I know a ghost when I see one. And we have them!"

"I thought ghosts were white or transparent," said Aleen, humoring him.

Ray made an exasperated noise. He had described the black shapes to Aleen a dozen times over. "Then what about all that other crazy shit going on? The lights, the TV, the f____ toaster, for Chrissakes!"

Aleen shrugged and kept her eyes on the dishes. "Get an electrician in. It's got to be the fuse box or some bad wiring."

Ray stomped out of the kitchen.

He went into the dining room. It was small but adequate in their raised ranch home. It was now dominated by a two-by-four-foot mirror framed in ornately carved cherry wood. Each corner had a fancy carved medallion.

They had found it at a yard sale about two weeks earlier. Aleen immediately wanted it, and it was cheap.

Ray stared into the mirror. An involuntary shiver went through him. Looking into it always gave him a creepy feeling.

Ray stared hard into the silvery surface. *Come on,* he thought, *I know you're in there. Show yourselves!*

The only images were his own agitated face and the dining room around him.

Ray went out for a ride to clear his mind.

The strange activity in the house was annoying from the start. Lights flickered as though the power was about to go out. Sometimes the lights in different rooms went completely off, then on. Sometimes Ray found a light on where he knew the light had been turned off. The kitchen appliances were not working right. The television went on by itself, and so did Ray's radio in the master bathroom.

It wasn't until Ray saw the shadow blobs that he linked the activity to the mirror. He was passing by the dining room and thought he saw dark movement out of the corner of his eye. When he looked, a tall, pillar-shaped black blob whisked to the mirror and sank into it, disappearing.

Ray thought it was his imagination—until he saw the same thing again. And again. The black blob—that's what Ray called it, a blob—was joined by several other blobs. There were seven of them altogether. He had the impression that they were intelligent and were aware that he noticed them. Crazy, yeah, but he could not deny what he felt.

Aleen remained oblivious. She commented on the electrical issues, but was convinced there was something wrong with the circuitry in the house. Ray did not mention the blobs, waiting to see if Aleen said something first.

She did not, so at last he broke his silence on them. She laughed it off as a vivid imagination.

Ray started spying on the blobs. He would rush into the dining room to see if he could catch them before they melted into the mirror. He would stare at the mirror for long periods of time, waiting for them to come out. They had to come out, he reasoned, if they went in. He never caught the black blobs coming out of the mirror—just going in.

The black blobs got bolder and started moving around the other rooms in the house. Sometimes Ray would be startled by one or more. Always, when he saw them, they glided at great speed toward the dining room. By the time Ray reached the dining room, they were usually gone—back into the mirror.

Something else started to happen to Ray that he did not talk about: strange dreams.

Somehow the blobs were getting into his dreams at night. He never saw them but he knew they were present, and they told him disturbing things. The blobs seemed to know all about his family and friends, and told him repeatedly that he could not trust his mother, sister, and two of his closest friends. The blobs said those people were out to get him.

Ray always awakened from the dreams upset, and with a queer feeling that something bad was going to happen to him. He could not shake it off.

When Ray got back from his ride, he felt clear-headed and knew he had to do something. He had already told Aleen he wanted to put the mirror out with the trash, but she would not hear of it. Since he did not want to deal with one of her Mt. Vesuvius anger acts, he let it go.

It was not long before he found John Zaffis. He told John what was going on in the house, and his suspicion that everything was tied into the mirror. He also told John about the dreams.

"You have a serious problem and we should take a look at it right away," John told him.

"I couldn't agree more," said Ray, relieved that he was not dismissed as a nutcase. "How soon can you get here?"

John arranged for an investigation with his team. Since the blobs moved around the house, he wanted to determine any other access points besides the mirror.

It was obvious to John as soon as he set foot in the house that an unusually charged atmosphere permeated the place. Aleen still did not notice much, but that's the way it is—different people tune in or tune out in their own way when paranormal activity is afoot. Some people are so sensitive that the slightest paranormal twitch registers on their Richter scale, while others have cement walls around them. Paranormal bombs could go off, and they wouldn't bat an eye.

John had his investigation team focus on the mirror. It radiated a strange vibe, the kind that only paranormal investigators are likely to sense after years of coming into contact with things that are not completely of this world.

"You're wasting your time," said Aleen as she watched the team set up their equipment. "There's nothing wrong with that mirror."

"We'll cover all the bases," said John, "if only to eliminate what is not the problem."

"Let them do their job," said Ray, annoyed.

"Is it true what Ray says, that black things or spirits disappear into the mirror?" persisted Aleen.

John nodded. "That's what we're going to try to find out. Actually, mirrors are well-known to be used as doorways by spirits and entities."

"Doorways? Into what? Where do they go, and where do they come from?" Aleen's tone was disbelief.

"Other dimensions," said John. "The spirit world is right beside us—we don't see it most of the time. Mirrors twist the psychic space and provide openings."

"Then I'm Alice wanting to go through the looking glass," said Aleen. "What's stopping *us* from going through mirrors?"

"We're not spirits," said John. "We have bodies."

Aleen threw up her hands. "Then everybody who owns a mirror should be haunted. Somebody call the newspaper! Headlines!" She spun on her heel to leave the dining room.

Ray looked at John. "You see what I have to put up with?"

John chuckled. He had seen this situation so many times he'd lost count. One person in a house experienced all or most of the paranormal phenomena, and others did not. If the non-experiencers were also disbelievers, then a war of sanity ensued.

After setting up around the mirror, the team spread out throughout the house to set up more equipment, take readings, and attempt to capture hard evidence. They worked for hours—and got nothing. Documenting the paranormal is never certain. Sometimes investigators can hit a gold mine and sometimes hit dust. It is rare, however, not to get a single EVP, which was the case that night. No one caught sight of the blobs, not even John, even though Ray piped up on several occasions and said he spotted them. The blobs did not show up in any photographs or video that were quickly reviewed on site.

Ray was crestfallen. "You guys didn't get nothin' hunh?"

"We don't know yet," John said as he packed up some of the gear. "Sometimes the evidence isn't obvious, and we only find it during a careful review. We'll go over what we got as soon as we can. In the meantime, it would be a good idea to take the mirror out of the house, or at least cover it up."

"Don't know that I can do that," said Ray. *"Her."*

After all the recordings, footage and other data were evaluated, John returned to the house to discuss the results and a proposed course of action with Ray and Aleen. There was little hard evidence—the blobs had kept themselves invisible—but the eyewitness accounts and experiences of Ray, as well as the other paranormal phenomena, were enough to diagnose the problem. The couple had a haunted mirror that was serving as a gateway for the blobs and possibly other spirits as well.

Ray, Aleen and John were the only persons in the house. They sat in the television room chatting, when suddenly a great commotion arose in another room. It sounded like pieces of furniture or heavy objects being roughly jerked about.

"That's coming from the dining room!" Ray shouted. He and John literally leaped off their seats and raced toward the room.

They found two dining chairs—which had been neatly tucked around the dining table—in crooked poses shoved up against the wall with the mirror. The chairs looked as though a giant hand had smacked them.

"Look!" Ray shouted as Aleen arrived behind them. "How do you explain *that*, Aleen?"

Aleen looked uncomfortable but said nothing.

"Looks like we finally got some action out of them," John said. He explained the concept of spirit attachment. "In certain cases, spirits can attach to objects, including mirrors. When the objects come into a home, the spirits start acting up, and they can throw furniture around. We don't know all of the history of this mirror, but somewhere along the line, it was attached. It looks like the kind of mirror that once was part of a dresser, so it may have been in someone's bedroom. If that person had an attachment, then the spirit could have transferred to the mirror at some point. When you bought the mirror, whatever was attached to it started activity in your house. It probably has caused the electrical activity you've noticed, and the dark forms. The mirror has become a doorway for spirits to enter into this world.

"What's different in this case," John added, "is that usually people see spirits in a mirror, or coming out of a mirror. You're seeing them go in."

"*He* is seeing them, not me," said Aleen, jabbing a thumb at Ray.

Ray ignored her. "That's what gets me," he said to John. "I never see them come out. They only go in, like a one-way street."

"They do come out," said John. "That's why you are having the other activity. They don't let you see them come out."

"This is just great," said Aleen. "I live in an effing Twilight Zone."

"Who are these black blobs?" asked Ray, still ignoring his wife. "Are they ghosts—dead people?"

"They're entities, probably trickster-type spirits," said John. "Those types of spirits can interfere in your dreams and cause ones like you've been having."

"What dreams?" demanded Aleen.

Ray sighed and told her.

Aleen's face creased into a scowl. "What's the matter with you? Are you trying to get rid of me by making me think you're crazy now? I swear Ray, maybe you *have* gone off the deep end!"

"Shut up, Aleen, you're not helping," Ray said. He looked at John. "Are they right—are they telling me the truth, something I should know? My mother, my family—I can't imagine not trusting any of them..." his voice trailed off.

"You probably know more than me on that score," John said. "I can tell you that tricksters like to play head games with people."

"I'm pulling out of this head game," said Ray. "Take the mirror with you if you want it. Otherwise, it will be in the garbage in the morning." He gave Aleen an icy look. "That's final, so shut your trap."

Ray did have the final word on the matter.

John slipped the mirror into his back seat and headed for home. He had not gone far when his radio acted up, scanning up and down the band as though an invisible hand were turning the dial. The volume shot up and a cacophony erupted at ear-splitting level.

At the same time, the car started bucking violently up and down. John had a hard time controlling the wheel. He managed to pull over onto the shoulder of the road.

John always travels with his "emergency kit" of holy water and sea salt. He had not treated the mirror while still at the home, but had taken it straight off the wall and into the car. The blobs evidently did not like their forced eviction.

John sprinkled the mirror with the holy water and sea salt, and said prayers over it. The radio stopped scanning, and the car quieted down. He made it the rest of the way home without further incident.

The mirror remained outside for a couple of days while John treated it again and performed a binding on it.

The removal of the mirror ended the activity in the home of Ray and Aleen. Ray was convinced they had experienced the supernatural, perhaps even something unholy. Aleen still remained uncertain that anything paranormal had occurred, even though she had no explanation for the dining chairs.

There was one thing that did not change: Ray's dreams. The mirror and the portal were gone, but "they" had wormed their way into his head, maybe into his very soul. The disturbing dreams continued, planting doubts about family and friends close to him, and warning him that something dire would happen to him.

After a few months, John heard that Ray and Aleen had separated. Their marriage had already been on precarious ground before the mirror came into the house, and the experience created another rift that added to their marital problems.

Ray became convinced that if he moved out of the house, he could banish the dreams. Aleen refused to move, and told him to go. He did.

Ray got an apartment. For a short time, he was free of the dreams, and he thought the link was finally severed. Then the dreams started up again.

Eventually, John lost touch with both Ray and Aleen. Two years went by, and then John received unsettling news: Ray had been killed in a freak motorcycle accident.

Were the blob dream voices right?

This case demonstrates the peculiar nature of haunting phenomena. The effects of a haunted object are not uniform. Ray was the focal point of all the activity created by the presence of the mirror, while his skeptical wife remained unaffected—and was even annoyed by Ray's insistence that paranormal phenomena were taking place.

Did the shadow blobs target Ray for a reason? Perhaps he was able to notice them while Aleen was not, and so his attention magnetized them.

Were the blobs trying to give Ray a warning? No evidence was found that Ray's family and friends did anything against him. He did, however, develop strong feelings of foreboding that something bad was going to happen to him. We can't directly connect these two phenomena, but they are part of a more complex picture.

Would Ray have had a premonition of his fatal accident in some other way if he had not acquired the mirror? There is no way to know for certain, and so we must leave it a mystery.

More common than seeing beings go in and out of mirrors is the manifestation of horrible faces in mirrors. John's Museum of the Paranormal has several mirrors that created havoc by showing demonic faces. Here are two cases:

Handle At Your Own Risk

One of the museum mirrors is small and round but packs a powerful paranormal punch. It is an ordinary, everyday mirror, the kind you might find in a variety store for cosmetic purposes. It has a cute little cartoon on one side of the frame, giving it a disarming, even charming, appearance. This mirror was far from charming, however—it was involved in a possession case that gravely affected a female victim. As demonic forces gained a stronger and stronger hold on the victim and her home, she found that the mirror was among the things affected. Whenever she looked into it, her face was transfigured into a horrible and ugly image.

The victim also felt the mirror had power over her, and she was compelled to look into it. She was nearly unable to tear away her gaze, despite being terrified by what she saw in the mirror.

Colleagues of John's handled the exorcisms and clearings with smudge, sea salt, holy water, and prayers. When the victim was finally freed from the demonic grip, she put the mirror in a cloth pouch to prevent accidentally seeing its surface. Strangely, she could not bring herself to get rid of the mirror, but she did not want to look into it either, out of fear that she would once again see the demonic image and the possession would come back on her.

The pouch was not enough protection for her, and soon she became convinced that even handling the pouch was dangerous. Finally she decided to turn it over to John. It was delivered with a note that read in part, "Caution: Do not look into the mirror and do not touch the pouch itself, only the purple string that is attached. Thank you for your help, God bless."

The mirror is now out of the pouch and no longer has the power to draw in the dark side.

The little round mirror is an example of an ordinary object that became contaminated by a demonic possession. When a dark force occupies an environment, it will take over and use whatever it can to create phenomena and gain a stronger grip on the victim. It is not known if the victim had subconscious superstitious beliefs about mirrors. If she did, they would have been an entry point for the demonic to take over and manipulate what she saw in the mirror.

The Demonic Mirror of Pat Reading

One of John's most extreme—and most famous—possession cases involved a woman, Pat Reading, of Litchfield, Connecticut, and her entire family. The case occurred in the 1980s and stretched over years. Pat endured excruciating tortures from invisible demonic assailants, and underwent 16 exorcisms performed by clergy. In the end, her health was broken, and she died of cancer in 2004. Her husband, Bill, and one daughter, Michelle, are gone now as well. The full story of Pat Reading will be shared in another book, but her demonic mirror is an excellent example of a haunted object.

Pat's demonic troubles started unexpectedly in 1988 when Pat was in her early fifties. She was living an ordinary life in the idyllic countryside, tending to home and family. Raised a Catholic, she had never had any remarkable encounters with the paranormal, or with supernatural forces.

One day while she was outside hanging laundry to dry, she was savagely attacked and raped by a mysterious assailant. Police were summoned, but the culprit was never identified or found. Instead, Pat later asserted that her attacker was no person, but a dark force.

That dark force was demonic, and it invaded the Reading household.

The first episode of strangeness occurred when a cup filled with tea tipped over, but none of the tea spilled out. Shocked, Pat could not fathom an explanation.

Other phenomena erupted. There was ongoing paranormal activity that increased and decreased and then increased again, involving unusual noises, foul smells, cold spots, apparitions and shadowy figures, and "possessed" objects that moved about on their own and radiated malevolent energy.

A demonic force took hold of Pat in full possession. She suffered breakdowns in which she collapsed, had seizures, got down on all fours and barked like a dog, and screamed and blasphemed. Sometimes it took multiple persons to hold her down. The breakdowns exhausted her physically, mentally, and spiritually, and her health declined.

John was among the experts who consulted on the case, which lasted for years. Pat trusted John completely and took him into her confidence. Eventually, Pat was freed of the dark force, but she spent the rest of her life holding up her guard against its return. Her legacy to John was her life story, and her two little dogs, who became John's cherished pets.

The maelstrom of activity that plagued the household involved a number of objects that were manipulated by the demonic force to ratchet up terror. Some of them, including the mirror, were items that Pat had acquired second hand. She and Bill loved to spend weekends hitting the neighborhood tag sales to scoop up bargains. It gave both of them a relief from the house, and for Pat, a special relief from the oppressive dark force that had a grip on her.

At one tag sale, Pat gravitated to an old mirror. It was a nice size, about 24 inches long by 18 inches wide, and Pat gauged that the frame might fit a photograph she had at home. From its distressed condition and carving style, Pat judged it to be Victorian in age. It was made of wood and stained dark brown. The stain was rubbed thin and completely off in many places. The silvering was deteriorated, and the mirror's surface was mottled with cloudy and dark spots. The backing on the mirror was crumbling.

This could be just the thing for that photo, she thought. Take out the mirror, clean up and repair the frame, add glass and she would have a great frame for her photograph.

Along with the mirror, she and Bill purchased two other items at the same tag sale: small knickknacks that were porcelain figures of women dressed in eighteenth- or nineteenth-century clothing.

Something changed by the time they arrived back home with their finds. As Pat took everything inside, she had a foreboding. Some of the items no longer felt right. She brought everything into the house, anyway.

She placed the knickknacks and mirror on an accent table and tended to household chores. When she returned to clean the mirror, she got an unexpected fright.

Pat was holding the mirror at an angle, wiping it down, when she saw the image of a pretty young woman in an old-fashioned dress reflected in it. The image was so life-like that for a split second she thought someone had entered the house and was standing behind her. She turned around, but no one was there. When she turned back to the mirror, the pretty woman was still there, but quickly transformed before Pat's very eyes into a horrible, demonic-looking hag.

Pat gasped and nearly dropped the mirror. A wave of nausea swept over her. She set the mirror down and walked rapidly away, heart pounding. "It" had gotten to her again! Did it take over the mirror or had she brought something else into her already-infested house?

She had to get the mirror out. Gingerly, Pat picked up the mirror, taking care not to look into its beaten-up silvered surface. She rushed outside and put it by a big beech tree in the backyard.

When she came back inside, Pat thought about the two knickknacks that had come from the same tag sale. They no longer looked right to her.

There was an evil presence clinging to them, waiting for the right moment to strike.

She picked up the figurines and rushed them outside to the tree, too.

Pat and Bill had an odd way of dealing with their possessions. Bill was a hoarder and never liked to throw anything out. His work space downstairs in the basement was full of stacks of boxes, items, and papers. It was hard to maneuver around everything. Stuff collected dust for years.

Pat felt a need to get rid of things, especially after the demonic activity started, but she would go only so far, and then she deferred to Bill. She put problem objects outside by the tree, and then asked Bill to dispose of them. Asking a hoarder to dispose of anything is like asking a person to stop breathing.

Perhaps this was how Pat subconsciously continued her role as a victim. The upshot was, haunted objects were allowed to continue to create problems even after they were identified as troublemakers.

So the mirror and knickknacks sat outside by the tree. Pat did feel relief as long as they were out of the house.

Daughter Michelle thought the mirror was cool and did not like to see it sit outside in the elements. One day she brought it back into the house while her mother was out on an errand. As soon as she did, paranormal activity kicked up. Wild banging sounded on the walls and the house felt like the inside of a pressure cooker.

Just then Pat came in, and was instantly alarmed by the noise and by Michelle holding the mirror.

"Stuff just started happening again," Michelle yelled over the commotion. "I don't know why!"

"It's the mirror," Pat shouted. "Why did you bring it back in the house? It's out there for a reason. Take it back outside!"

Michelle took the mirror outside, and the phenomena in the house subsided.

One day the mirror disappeared from beside the tree. Pat assumed that Bill had finally thrown it out. The figurines were still there. Maybe he had forgotten them.

Bill had not disposed of the mirror, however, but had sneaked it down to his basement workshop. He liked the frame and thought he might have a use for it—someday.

The house became active again, with unpleasant phenomena that would not stop. Pat had no idea what triggered the activity, until Bill confessed to having brought the mirror back into the house.

Pat was furious. Back out the mirror went. She called John.

When John arrived, he found all three objects—the mirror and the figurines—tossed out by the tree.

Pat told him what had been happening. "I don't know if there was something in the mirror, or the mirror was being affected by the house," she said.

"Sometimes it's hard to separate the two," said John, examining the mirror. "This has a human attachment to it, but it also could be manipulated by the forces that are present in the house. It could be a combination of the two."

"Please take it away," said Pat. "Take the figurines, too. They all came from the same place."

Unfortunately, neither Pat nor Bill could remember the property where they had purchased the items. They had spent the entire day going from one tag sale to another, and they all blurred together. Thus, there was no opportunity to investigate the background history of the afflicted objects.

John gave the objects a cleansing and binding, and made special prayers for the attached soul to send it on its way to the light. He then bound the mirror to prevent anything demonic that was attached to it from acting up.

The mirror was only one of many objects to frighten Pat over the years of her demonic ordeal. Not everything in the house was affected, but if objects with the "right" energy were introduced from another environment, they became the devil's tools in Pat's home.

The mystery of mirrors

Mirrors have always had a connection to the spirit realm, and have been used since ancient times to communicate with the dead, summon spirits, see the future, and reveal the truth. Their supernatural history is a checkered one, marked by the good and the bad.

Ever since Narcissus caught sight of his reflection in water and could not tear himself away, people have been drawn to mirrored surfaces. Gazing into a shiny, smooth surface opens the doorways between dimensions. For millennia, people have used whatever reflective surface is at hand: water in dark ponds or bowls; fingernails and palms of the hand covered with oil and soot; metals and polished stones and crystals; and mirrors made of bronze, brass, stones, crystals, silvered glass, and black glass.

Mirrors can act as portals for the dead and spirits. Many of those beliefs sprang from times when few people had mirrors, and so they were a mysterious and exotic item. The depth of their reflective surfaces seemed to penetrate into unknown and possibly dangerous territory.

Folklore beliefs around the world caution of a mirror's effect on the newly dead. Back in the days when corpses were laid out at home for wakes and viewing prior to burial, people covered or turned over all the mirrors in the house. It was believed that the dead lingered by their bodies until burial, and if they saw themselves in a mirror, they would become disoriented and perhaps not leave with their bodies when removed for burial. If that happened, then they became stuck and would haunt a home—quite unhappily.

The living were not immune, either. If the living saw a corpse reflected in a mirror, it meant their souls would be carried off by the ghosts of the dead.

Other folklore beliefs have held that mirrors were gateways for the devil or demons, or would steal souls. It was once a common practice for mirrors to be covered or turned around in a room or even entire house where a person was ill. It was unlucky for the sick to see their reflections while they were in a weakened state.

If mirrors could usher in, then mirrors could usher out, and many folklore practices also developed for using mirrors to deflect the unwanted, including malevolent witches and sorcerers as well as spirits. The ancient art of placement known as feng shui, developed in China around 4000 BC, utilizes mirrors for protection and for modifying and deflecting harmful flows of natural energy around and through houses and buildings.

In magic, mirrors have been used to summon spirits and even trap them "inside" the mirrors. If such a mirror passes ownership with the spirit still inside, there is a risk of the spirit breaking loose in a new environment. It will not be happy about its imprisonment, and will take out its anger upon the new owners.

On the other side of the coin, many people have positive, even healing experiences with mirrors, especially when they use them for communicating with the dead. Mirrors—especially black mirrors—make excellent tools for contact with the dead and spirits, for developing clairvoyance, navigating the astral plane, and looking into past lives. If mirrors are used properly, they pose no problem.

Sometimes, however, mirrors are trouble. People use them to open the wrong door—or, they forget to close the door they opened, and the invited become the uninvited. Sometimes mirrors get activated by other paranormal phenomena that start up around them.

We have seen mirrors figure in many problem hauntings. If an unwelcome presence has latched on in a household, badly placed mirrors can make the situation worse. Mirrors in bedrooms are especially problematic. Mirrors should not be positioned so that a person can see himself in bed. A mirror should not be at the foot or side of the bed, or over the head of the bed.

Many people sleep with mirrors in their bedrooms and suffer no ill effects, even when mirrors cover the sliding doors of closets that parallel the bed. To be on the safe side, however, be mindful of mirrors.

In addition, mirrors should never reflect into each other, even at distant angles. A mirror in one room of a house should not look into a mirror in a hallway or other room, or elsewhere in the same room. This configuration seems to widen the opening between dimensions.

Should you be concerned about a second hand mirror? Pay attention to clues and cues. If you have a "funny feeling" about a mirror, pass it by.

7

The Ritual Robe

The black hooded robe draped over a mannequin in the window display was perfect, just what Steve was looking for. Halloween was fast approaching, and he didn't yet have his costume for the round of campus parties.

He went inside and fingered the robe. It was not cheap and flimsy, but made of a heavy, felted fabric. He turned over the price tag and got sticker shock. Wow! Pricey for a Halloween getup.

"That's a real antique," said a male voice behind him.

Steve turned around to a middle-aged, beetle-browed man with round spectacles and a faint smile on his face. "It's not a costume?" he asked.

"Yes, in a way," the man answered. "This is a real robe that was worn for rituals. It's about a century old. Made of wool. You won't find another like it anytime soon."

"Rituals? What sort of rituals?"

The man raised his shoulders slightly. "Who knows. It's the kind of robe worn by ritual magicians in the past. Your guess is as good as mine as to what they did in it." He leaned closer. "Maybe conjured demons, you know what I mean?"

"Yeah, maybe," said Steve, now quite intrigued by the robe. "How do you know for sure that it was used in magic?"

The man ran his fingers down the robe. "This came from the estate of someone who was very—and I mean *very*—interested in the occult. There were other things, too—tools, jewelry, objects. They're all sold now, except for the robe." He looked Steve in the eye. "It takes the right person to wear this."

"Hey, I'm not a wizard," Steve said. "I just want a costume for Halloween."

The man smiled. "Would you like to try it on?" He had the garment off the mannequin before Steve could answer, and slipped it over Steve's shoulders.

The robe was heavy. Steve had the sudden sensation of feeling as old as the robe, as though he were being swept back in time.

The man ushered him to a mirror. Steve liked what he saw. Yes, very imposing, especially with his dark hair and dark looks. He squinted and tried to look sinister. There were all sorts of possibilities with this: executioner, bad priest, sorcerer, witch hunter, mad alchemist. Not to mention the attention he would get with a real, old ritual robe.

"Would you like to take it home?" the man's words broke in on Steve's thoughts.

Steve hesitated. As much as he wanted the robe, it was expensive. "It's a lot of money for a costume," he said.

The man smiled. His eyes looked huge behind his spectacles. "I'm sure we can accommodate you. After all, it has been here a while. And it does seem perfect for you." He offered a surprisingly low price.

"I can manage that," said Steve, nodding. *Awesome.*

Home was a dorm room pod on a college campus that Steve shared with three other young men. He proudly showed off his trophy to his roommates.

"Check this out, dudes—this is a real magician's robe, a hundred years old!"

"Nice," one said. "What was it worn for—roasting babies and worshiping Satan?" They all laughed.

"Yeah, why don't you carry one of those bloody demon baby dolls?" They all laughed again.

Steve hung the robe in his tiny closet. He decided he would go to the parties as a sorcerer. He would pick up a few more costume items to make the look complete.

The dorm pod's four private rooms clustered around a common area with a kitchen, eating and sitting area, and bathroom. Each private room had a twin bed, a closet, and a small desk. Steve did not know any of his roommates prior to the start of the school year. They all got along fairly well, although their personal habits sometimes clashed. One of the four, Winston, was the ultra-studious type and was always asking the night owls to tone it down. Another roommate, Ron, was a party guy who stayed out late a lot, and crashed around when he came in. The third roommate, Michael, was influenced by Ron. Steve was in the middle—he tried to get along with everyone.

It was about 2 AM that night when Steve finished studying and turned off his light and iPod. He could see under the crack in his door that the common area was dark, indicating that his roommates had also turned in or were out.

He was just drifting off when there was a terrible crash in the common area. It sounded like metal pots and pans clanging on the floor. He jumped up and yanked open his door.

All the lights were on in the common area, blinding bright. Pots were scattered over on the floor. A lid was still rolling on its edge.

The other three doors had also been flung open, and all the roommates were shouting.

"What the f___'s going on?"

"Who the hell did that?"

The cabinets in the little kitchen were wide open. The young men did not have much in the way of dishes and utensils, but every pot and pan in the cupboard was now lying on the floor.

It took several minutes for the confusion to abate, as each roommate disavowed any role in the incident.

"Then how did this happen?" challenged Winston. "These pans didn't fly out of the cupboard by themselves!" he looked at Ron in an accusatory way.

"Hey, I had nothing to do with this, derp," Ron said.

"Hold on, all you guys," Steve said. "Let's get things back together." He started picking up the pans and lids. "They must have been stacked to push on the cabinet doors, and the doors just came open." He knew it was lame.

"*All* of them?" said Winston.

Steve shrugged.

The young men returned to their rooms. As Steve turned out the lights in the common area, it dawned on him that there was also no explanation for how they got turned on. He was the first one to open his door, and the lights were already on. The others must have assumed that he turned them on.

Steve felt uncomfortable, but he told himself it was all a freak incident.

There were more freak incidents in the days and nights to come. Lights in the pod developed minds of their own, going on and off without human touch. Water faucets in the kitchen and bathroom were found running when no one was present.

Winston suggested they call maintenance to investigate. "It's getting damned annoying," he said. "I don't know why this place has turned into a haunted house all of a sudden. I know it is Halloween, but it's *not funny.*"

One morning three of them were in the pod. Michael was in the shower. Suddenly a scream came from the bathroom. Michael, dripping wet with a towel clutched to his middle, tore out, spewing a stream of expletives.

The water had suddenly turned from hot to icy cold.

Later the same day, Steve returned from class to find his room trashed. Steve was not the neatest person, but this was a hit job. The outer door to the pod was usually locked, but Steve was not in the habit of locking his personal door. No one in the pod did.

His bedding was in a pile on the floor. His clothes were strewn about. Papers that had been sitting on his desk were scattered everywhere.

Steamed, he assumed it was a Halloween prank perpetrated by one of his roommates, probably Ron. That guy was always up to something.

Soon it was discovered that all the rooms had been trashed. The students fell into a heated argument, accusing each other. Although the blame could be pinned on none of them, they all remained suspicious of each other.

More objects in the pod were affected. Sounds of dishes and glasses breaking shattered the night.

It became evident that none of the roommates were responsible for any of the mischief; nor could they find any outsiders to blame. None of the other occupants of the building had reported break-ins. Why were they being singled out?

"We've got a ghost," said Winston. "I don't know why, but that's the only explanation."

"Real bright, Einstein," said Ron.

"Maybe we should try to make contact with it," said Michael. "Do a séance or something."

"A Ouija board," suggested Steve.

Steve purchased a Ouija board at a second hand shop in town. They waited until dark and then put the board out on the kitchen table, along with a candle Steve had also bought. Steve and Winston were elected to operate the pointer while Ron and Michael looked on.

"You put your fingers on it real light," said Ron. "Don't push. The ghost is supposed to do the talking."

"What if a demon comes out of the board and starts killing us?" said Michael.

"That's a movie, dumb ass," said Winston. "Nobody is going to get killed."

"What do we ask?" said Steve.

"If anyone is here," said Ron. "A name. Whatever."

"Okay. Someone ask the questions." Steve put his fingertips on the pointer. Winston followed suit.

"I'll ask," said Ron. He cleared his throat. "Is anybody here?"

The pointer did not move.

"Is anybody here?" Ron repeated. "Talk to us."

Slowly, the pointer inched to YES, to the excitement of the witnesses.

"It's not me," said Steve. "I'm not doing a thing!"

"Me neither," said Winston.

The pointer stopped when it reached YES and stayed there.

"All right," said Ron. "Give us a name. Spell it."

Slowly, the pointer meandered around the board, not stopping on any letter or word.

"Spell your name," said Ron.

The pointer stopped on a string of consonants, not making sense. They tried several times to get a name, and then gave up.

"Are you the one who's been messing around with us?" asked Ron. "The lights, the dishes and everything?"

The pointer moved to YES.

"Who *are* you?"

The pointer remained motionless.

For the remainder of the Ouija session, the pointer wandered aimlessly around the board in response to every question.

"Tell it to go away, whatever it is," said Winston.

"Why me?" said Ron.

"Because you're asking the questions and it's listening to you."

"All right." Ron looked at the board as though it were the ghost. "We want you to go away and stop bothering us. Will you go away?"

"The pointer began to move. But it did not move up to YES, or to NO. Instead, it moved to GOODBYE.

The session with the Ouija board made the situation worse. That night the poltergeist activity increased, and a heavy, oppressive feeling crept over the entire pod. No more pots were thrown about, but instead heavy banging sounded on the walls. There were yowling sounds, as though cats were fighting. The four roommates were alarmed now, but had no idea what to do.

"Maybe if we ignore it, it will go away," Michael suggested the next day. They agreed on that as a plan of action.

The night of the first Halloween party arrived. Steve put on black jeans, a black tee and the robe, and topped it with some magical pendants on long silver-colored chains that he had bought at a costume shop. Though the robe was wool, he felt chilled as soon as he put it on. And dizzy. Weird.

At the party, he felt oddly disconnected. He swam through thick air. Voices sounded far away. Even the admiration of others over his real ritual robe did not offset his disorientation.

More alarming were flashes of visions of someplace else. All of a sudden, the room around him was transposed to another scene. He was inside an unfamiliar building, standing in a circle with strange men dressed in dark robes similar to his. His surroundings were lit by torches and candles, but he could not see beyond the circle. Strange symbols decorated the floor inside the circle. He heard faint chanting. He was both himself and could see himself. It looked like a ritual.

The visions were fleeting, so fast he thought it was his imagination. But as the evening wore on, he felt as though he were someone else, walking in someone else's shoes.

He went home early.

Steve decided that he was merely creeped out by everything that had been going on in the dorm. It did not occur to him that there was any connection between the activity and the robe.

The next night, he wore the robe to another party. The same things happened again. He was immediately cold to the bone as soon as he put the robe on. The same visions flashed on him, this time stronger and longer.

He did not enjoy the party and went back to the dorm early again.

The queasy feeling lifted from him when he took off the robe. At that moment, he realized there was something very, very wrong with the robe. Now all the dots were connected.

Steve was so distraught that he excused himself from school and went home to his parents' house, where he remained an entire week in a disconnected state of mind. He told his mother, Barbara, he was not feeling well, but he could not describe the obvious symptoms of any illness. Worried, she thought stress of school might be affecting him, and he was having a nervous breakdown.

Finally, Steve confessed to Barbara his fears about the robe, and that it had a hold on him. "I haven't worn it since that last party," he said. "But I don't feel like myself anymore."

Barbara was alarmed. The family was Catholic, and she relied upon her religious upbringing. She saw the dark forces of the devil at play. "You must go see the priest," she said, referring to the parish priest.

Steve was reluctant, but Barbara insisted.

Steve told the priest everything that had happened. The priest agreed that dark forces were at work. The agents of the devil could take hold of objects and affect people. If the robe had been worn for dark purposes, such as spirit summoning, then the effects could have rubbed off on Steve. The priest said prayers over Steve—but he refused, without reason, to go to the campus dorm room, where the robe still hung in the closet.

The next call was made to John.

It was not the first time that John had heard of clergy declining to become involved in a paranormal situation. Many times over the years he had worked closely with different clergy. Some, however, declined to intervene. They, too, had their thresholds concerning hostile spirits.

When contacted by Steve, John agreed to act quickly. By the time people reach out to someone for help, their situation usually has escalated to an unbearable level. Relief is important, as well as breaking the hold of the source of the problem before it acquires more strength.

John removed the robe and treated the dorm pod with holy water and sea salt. He did an immediate binding on the robe.

"This is an authentic ritual robe," he told Steve. "Whoever owned and wore this robe used it to summon spirits, because I can detect both human and spirit energy attached to it. It's so old that it probably was worn by more than one person, so there may have been many purposes involved."

"What do you mean by human energy?" Steve asked. "A dead person is attached?"

"It's residual, the energy left behind by a person when they die. Magic rituals require very high levels of emotional energy and concentration. When rituals are done over and over again for years, a residue of that energy sticks to the clothing. It might be inactive for years once the clothing is no longer worn, but when someone uses it again, it gets recharged, and you have paranormal activity.

"Then you've got the spirits, too," John continued. "When spirits are summoned over and over, they can become attached to a person, especially if they are not sent away properly. They can jump to objects, even clothing. I think that's what happened with your robe."

"Did those people I saw in the visions summon demons?" Steve looked worried.

"There are all kinds of spirits summoned in magic," John said. "Some of them are tricksters, and if they get a chance, they will cause problems—like the ones you had."

John visited the shop where Steve had purchased the robe, but the man who sold it was sharp and unfriendly, and claimed to have no knowledge of any magical purpose or history concerning the robe. "It's nothing more than an old piece of clothing," he said with a dismissive gesture. "Probably some old coach coat. People bring in their old clothes all the time, things they find in the attic or in a relative's estate. I think the boy has an overactive imagination."

John knew better, but he let the matter ride. The case was solved, anyway.

With the removal of the robe and the blessings on Steve, the activity ceased. Steve soon felt normal again. He told John he never wanted anything more to do with the paranormal. "Next year I'm going to stick to the costume shops for Halloween," he said.

Several weeks later, John received a large box in the mail. It was the Ouija board and pointer. A handwritten note said, "Hi Mr. Zaffis. We don't want this, either. Steve."

The ritual robe joins other items of clothing in the Museum of the Paranormal. Some are ordinary, everyday pieces of clothing. An item does not have to have been used in magical rituals in order to have attachments or residues. Secondhand clothes that were favorites of their original owners may retain strands of residual energy. The energy may not always cause unpleasant phenomena, but may be picked up by the new wearer, who tunes in to the original owner, perhaps with flashes of scenes from that person's life, or personal memories.

Objects, including clothing, that have been regularly used in occult work are bathed in energies from the spirit world and the presence of spirits. Magical work is not inherently bad; some people use magic for benevolent spell casting and personal spiritual work. Other people open the door to the dark side, looking for spirits that will serve materialistic purposes. The spirit energy attached to the robe was of a dark nature. It manifested destructive phenomena and played games on the Ouija.

The students were well-intentioned to attempt to discover the source of the phenomena, but they picked the wrong tool for the job. The Ouija, as we've noted, is often easily manipulated by spirits. Using the board and inviting the spirit to communicate gave it even more energy to be destructive.

When paranormal activity gets out of hand, pull back and get help.

8

The Not So Angelic Cherub

Love, once broken, can never be put back together again. Some people, however, never get over a lost love and will go to strange lengths to try to recover it. They have to learn the hard way.

Al was one of those persons.

Ever since Sherry left him, Al felt his life was empty and meaningless. He knew he should heal his wounds and move on, and was always trying to convince himself that he was on the verge of rebirth. After every burst of energy, he sank back into depression. No other woman interested him. Sherry had been the best. How could he have lost her?

The two of them had had a great thing going, he told himself. They were perfect for each other. Al had even entertained the thought of proposing. Then Sherry blew apart the universe by telling him that she had met someone else and wanted to make it exclusive with him. And that was that.

After Al came out of shell shock, he was angry. What did Sherry see in this other guy that was so great? Okay, so he was wealthy. She probably was blinded by his big bank account. Maybe she wasn't so worthy after all, if she was mesmerized by money.

No, that wasn't it. Sherry had more substance than that. There had to be something else.

Soon Al was crazy with jealousy.

He tried talking to Sherry. She gently but firmly told him that all was well, and she was committed to her new relationship. In fact, things were going exceptionally well. She hoped Al was over their breakup and back on his feet.

"Oh yes," he lied. "I'm doing fine, even seeing someone I really like. I just wanted to make sure you were all right."

But Al was not doing fine.

Months went by, and Al went through the motions of living. Then he received another body blow to the heart: Sherry had married Mr. Rich Guy.

The Flood, the Apocalypse, and the End Times were scenarios that all paled by comparison to the end of Al's personal world.

He kept telling himself it couldn't last. Sherry would soon see the error of her ways. She would ditch Mr. Rich Guy, and when she did, Al would be in the wings waiting.

The grapevine of mutual friends reported a much different situation. Sherry and her new husband were wildly happy. They were building a spectacular new house. Sherry wanted to start a family soon.

Al moped and mulled and obsessed on getting Sherry back, even though she was receding from him at the speed of light. Then he hit on a plan: magic.

Magic was real, wasn't it? People had been casting spells for centuries, even millennia, so something about it must work. He just had to figure out how. If he could put a spell on Sherry to pull her back, then once she was out of her husband's clutches she would indeed see the error of her ways and realize Al was the Mr. Right Guy all along.

Al visited an occult bookstore and came home with shopping bags full of books on magical spells. He spent hours online reading websites. He was soon overwhelmed—magic was a complicated matter, more than reciting a spell. Perhaps he should hire someone to do it for him.

Al located such a person, a woman who advertised help for those who wished to find love, get money, improve their health, and in general enhance their lives. Her name was Rhianna.

Al expected to find someone dressed like a Gypsy in a parlor full of velvet and tie-dyed curtains. Instead he found an ordinary-looking woman dressed in everyday clothes. That was disappointing, but okay as long as she could do the job.

He announced that he wanted to get his old love back.

Rhianna nodded. "Do you have a photograph of her?"

Al produced one. It was a bit ragged and dog-eared from being carried constantly in his shirt pocket.

"What happened? Did you have a fight?"

Al explained how they broke up and then Sherry got married.

Rhianna handed him back the photograph, shaking her head. "I help people find true love, I help people improve their relationships, I help estranged lovers get back together, but I don't break up marriages."

"But—"

"Sorry."

So Al went back to his solo drawing board.

He figured out his plan of attack. To cast a good spell, it was best to make something by hand, and to have something personal of the recipient. Al had nothing personal of Sherry's but he would make a gift for her, something she would definitely want to keep.

She had always been fond of angels and cherubs, and had numerous art prints of them gracing her apartment. Al figured he could draw one. That would make the gift more personal and important.

He found a nice drawing and rendered a rough copy in the form of a large black-and-white cherub. While he drew, he repeated a spell he had composed for Sherry to think about him and want to come back to him. He also gazed at his photograph of her while he worked, mentally transferring her into the drawing.

When finished, the cherub was crude compared to the original. A bit out of proportion, but never mind. For some reason, Al had been inspired to give the cherub solid black eyes, like two marbles, and a slight smile with a finger held to the mouth as if to say, *shhh...* In the other hand, down at the side, was a heart.

To Al, the cherub looked quite appealing.

Next step: delivery.

Sherry was not pleased to get the phone call from Al proposing a lunch date at their former favorite restaurant. "Thank you for the invitation and that's very sweet of you, Al, but I really don't think it would be appropriate."

"But it's my birthday next week," he wheedled. "Come on, just for old time's sake. I'd love to hear how things are going. Besides, I have something for you. I never gave you a wedding present, you know."

"Well—"

"Oh, come on, it can't hurt. We can still be friends, can't we?"

Against her better judgment, Sherry agreed.

She arrived at the restaurant determined to make lunch as short as possible. Al was already seated and waiting for her. His face beamed as she approached. He stood up to greet her. He looked scrubbed and shiny, though thinner than when she had last seen him.

Sherry gave him a tight smile and a fleeting hug, avoided a kiss, and sat down.

Al was animated. As he talked Sherry marveled to herself, *He's acting like we're still together, like nothing ever happened.* She turned the topic to her husband, but it made no dent in him. Al listened with a smile pasted on his face.

After the wheels of time ground through eternity, they were at the end of the meal, sipping the last of their coffee.

"I saved the best for last," Al said, and reached down to a bag at the side of his chair. He pulled out a large flat parcel wrapped in silver and white paper and tied with a silver bow. He handed it to Sherry. "For you."

"Oh," Sherry said awkwardly.

"Go ahead, open it."

She peeled off the paper. When she saw the cherub, she could not believe Al would give something like that to her—not because it was beautiful, but because it was… *awful.*

Sherry forced a smile. "Thank you, Al."

He grinned. "I drew it myself."

Sherry wondered, *Is this a joke? He can't possibly think I would find this attractive.*

As if he read her mind, Al said, "I know, who knew I could draw? Not bad, eh? You love cherubs, so… what better than to make one for you? A little memento from me to you!"

He sat there grinning with his mouth full of teeth, and Sherry did not have the heart to tell him she did not like it at all.

"I know just where I will put this," she said. And that was the truth.

Back home, Sherry left the cherub on the parlor table until her husband, Eagan, got home. She showed it to him.

"I think Al is still carrying a torch for me," she said.

Eagan creased his brow. "I'd like to put a torch to *that*." He looked down at the drawing. "That's got to be the ugliest cherub I ever saw. It looks more like a demon."

"I'll put it in the basement."

Sherry took the cherub and went downstairs. She placed it on top of a packing box. *Unbelievable,* she thought.

The cherub stared at her. Its grin was more like a smirk. The black eyes looked malevolent. Eagan was right—it was more a demon than a cherub.

She went back upstairs and left the cherub in the dark, already nearly forgotten.

Sherry may have easily forgotten the cherub, but she found that she could not forget Al. Since having lunch with him, she could not get him off her mind. She mentally replayed the lunch date, and then reminisced about their relationship. She thought about Al all the time, like a teenager with a crush.

She could not understand it. She loved Eagan, was blissfully happy. She had enjoyed her relationship with Al, but he had always been more of a friend to her than a romantic interest. Why was she thinking so much about him now?

Even more peculiar, Sherry started dreaming about Al nearly every night. Some of the dreams were sexual in nature—and, she secretly admitted to herself, quite pleasurable. She felt guilty.

One day Sherry was rummaging through her drawers and spied a box that she knew contained pieces of gold jewelry Al had given her while they were dating. She had never been able to bring herself to get rid of them, but she hadn't felt right wearing them, either. They were lovely pieces, set with semi-precious stones. Al really did have good taste, in spite of the hideous drawing.

Sherry started wearing the jewelry. It made Al feel even closer to her.

Eagan was not pleased when he found out where the jewelry came from. "What's going on, Sherry? Are you seeing him?" he demanded.

"Of course not! I found them in a drawer and I thought it would be nice to wear them. They don't mean anything to me, and I'm *not* seeing Al!"

Sherry wore Al's jewelry a lot, even when she and Eagan went out to dinner. They fought about it every time.

Their fighting increased. Sherry and Eagan no longer got along smoothly, but argued about everything, big and small. When they did, Sherry found herself thinking wistfully about Al, and all the good times they had shared.

Unusual things happened in the house. When the tension was high, or when the couple fought, something would break on its own. A vase mysteriously fell off a shelf. Dishes not even near the edge of a counter rolled off onto the floor and smashed. The house took on a heavy air. At night, Sherry sometimes awakened to hear odd noises, as though someone were moving around. The alarm system never tripped, however. A few times, she roused Eagan to investigate. He grew irritated with her "wild imagination," and so she stopped waking him. Instead, she lay frozen in fear beneath the covers.

Sherry forgot all about the cherub until she went down to the basement one evening, and saw it on top of the packing box. It was still as ugly as ever. The cherub looked like he was up to no good. But she could not throw the drawing away.

Sherry did not associate her fixation on Al with the activity in the house, but she did wonder if the house had become haunted. If it was, she wanted it to stop. A friend recommended that she call John. He made an appointment to see her. Eagan was present as well.

In interviewing people about their paranormal situations, John always looks beyond the paranormal incidents to other personal life factors. The source of activity often lies in the human world and not the spirit world. Important factors include strained and dysfunctional relationships; emotional trauma and upheaval; financial and health problems; substance abuse; and occult interests. All of these can create turmoil that draws in spirit activity. In some cases, people project their problems into the environment. The "haunting" has natural causes, and the personal issues have to be addressed. In yet other cases, there are combinations of all of these factors.

John knew immediately that there was more to the story than haunting phenomena. There was obvious tension between Sherry and Eagan, and he asked a few questions to get them to talk about it.

"Why don't you ask her about the necklace she's wearing," snapped Eagan.

Sherry haltingly explained that she was wearing an old flame's jewelry, but had no explanation as to why.

The jewelry was too old to account for the recent problems, thought John. "Did you bring anything into the house at about the time the activity started?" he asked.

Sherry thought a moment. "No... oh, wait a minute! That cherub!" She told John about the lunch date and the gift of the creepy cherub with the coal black eyes. She admitted that after the lunch, she had started thinking about Al a great deal, even dreaming about him.

Sherry led John downstairs to the basement. He examined the drawing. "Is your old boyfriend into the occult? I think he did a spell on you and put it into this drawing."

Sherry was aghast. "I don't see how that could be true, but I will get to the bottom of it," she said. She gave the drawing to John. "If Al really did that, then I don't want this anywhere near me."

John cleansed and bound the drawing to break the spell, and stowed it in the Museum of the Paranormal. In a few days, he received a call from Sherry.

"I confronted Al," she said. "At first he denied everything, but he finally admitted that he had tried putting a love spell on the drawing. Ever since we broke up, he has been hoping I would come back to him. When it was obvious I was moving on with my life—even getting married—he got desperate." She paused. "Do love spells really work?"

"If someone tries to force love, no, not in the long run," John answered. "You can't force someone to do something against their will. I have seen some forced love spells that have a temporary effect, and the person who does the spell thinks they are going to get what they want. In the end, they lose. Something always goes wrong. The spells can still cause a lot of trouble until they backfire."

"I guess that does explain why suddenly I was thinking about Al so much, and having dreams about him. Even going back to wearing the jewelry that he gave me. By the way, I got rid of all those pieces."

"That's good," said John. "Spells work on emotional connections, so anything that has an emotional connection to Al can create a link to this sort of activity."

"Do you think Al will try something like this again?"

"Sometimes people do try again, but I think he got the message," said John. "He's better off putting all that energy into finding a new relationship. And how are things with the husband?"

Sherry sighed. "It took Eagan a while to accept that I wasn't myself while all this was going on. He doesn't believe in the paranormal, or spells. But since we got rid of everything—especially that awful drawing—the house has been quiet and comfortable again. I feel like my old self, too."

"Great to hear that. Okay, call me if anything else happens."

There were no more calls. The not so angelic cherub was put out of action, but there is still plenty of mischievous glint in the coal black eyes. Is there such a thing as a "demonic angel"? If so, this might be the first ever portrait of one.

The cherub joins many other objects in the museum that were once ritually imbued with love spells, all with disastrous results. Unrequited love, jealous love, bleeding hearts, and revenge drive some people to extreme measures to claim or reclaim the person of their desire, or hurt them if they cannot. As noted in this case, love cannot be forced. There are many ways to attract the right love, enhance love, and even repair love. Prayers, affirmations, and visualizations are part of metaphysical approaches to manifest what you want and improve what you have. Love cannot be twisted, however, and anything aimed at destroying a relationship in order to seize someone is morally and ethically wrong. Hopefully Al learned his lesson.

There was a lesson for Sherry as well: to pay more attention to her intuition. She should have declined the gift on the spot, which she could have done gracefully. She didn't want to hurt Al's feelings—but he did not have her best interests at heart, only his own.

9

Mr. Sinister Finds A New Home

One of Patrick's favorite pastimes on a sunny weekend day was strolling through the local flea markets where he lived, looking for the odd find. Over the years, he had acquired a quirky collection of things that had no unified theme, but had captured his fancy of the moment. Patrick lived alone and had no one to please but himself, and he did just that.

On this sunny and humid summer day, the pickings were slim. Patrick walked slowly up and down the aisles of tables and booths, his practiced eye roving over the jumbles of merchandise for sale. Some days were bonanzas and some were busts, and this one was shaping up as a bust.

He was about to call it quits when his eye fell on a strange statue made of carved wood. It was a man about three-and-a-half feet tall, dressed in a long-sleeved, collarless shirt and pants. He had red eyes and wore an odd headdress that looked like a large crescent. He held a stick in one hand and clutched something to him in the other. His expression was somber. To Patrick, a big fan of the offbeat, the statue oozed charm.

Charm indeed—more like the devil's charm.

Late in the day, close to closing time, the bargains at flea markets get better. Patrick easily haggled a low price on the figure. In fact, it seemed that the vendor was eager to get rid of it.

As soon as Patrick picked up the statue, a strange tingling shot through his body, as though he'd touched a light socket. He shrugged it off, thinking it had to do with the thunderclouds that were building in the western sky. He carried the statue out to his car and opened the trunk, where he always kept a blanket or two for the unexpected find. As he carefully arranged the blankets around it, he could not ignore a feeling of profound unease and foreboding that swept over him. He shrugged that off, too.

Patrick decided to put the weird man inside his house rather than outside. He positioned it by the sliding glass door to his patio. The figure leered at him.

The next day, Patrick awakened to a foul smell that permeated the house. Had he forgotten to take out the garbage? He checked the kitchen waste bin, but it had been recently emptied. Was there a smell of rotting food in the refrigerator was that seeping out? He checked the fridge but found nothing that could account for the odor. He searched for other possible sources, and even checked outside to see if something was leaking in. Nothing. The air outside was fresh and clean.

Perhaps something died behind a wall, like a mouse.

Patrick aired out the house and sprayed a freshener, and left for work.

When he returned that evening, the stink was back, and worse. Exasperated, Patrick again searched for the offending source, but could find nothing.

He went to the patio door to open it, and as he neared the statue, that strange electrical feeling shot through his body again. How odd.

As the evening progressed, Patrick felt nauseated. He thought perhaps he had eaten something that had spoiled enough to make him sick. He downed some anti-acid but felt no better. Instead, he sank into a black depression. The foul smell in the house added to his nausea. Soon he went to bed and tossed and turned all night. He got up twice to vomit.

The house still stank in the morning. Patrick went to the patio door to sit outside. Maybe some fresh air would help him.

When he neared the statue, the tingling shot through him.

Now he knew it was no coincidence—something happened every time he got near the statue. He backed away and then approached it again. Zap!

Patrick reached out and gingerly touched the man on the cap. *Zap!* He stared down at the statue. Was it his imagination, or was the somber face twisted into a leer?

Suddenly a shock hit Patrick: There was something wrong with the statue. Horribly wrong.

It occurred to him that there was a spirit inhabiting the statue, even animating its face to change expression. He had heard of such things. And for reasons unknown, the statue did not like him.

As soon as the realization hit, Patrick scooped up the statue and placed it outside on the patio. He slammed the sliding door shut and heaved out a sigh.

With the weird man out of the house, the environment improved. The foul smell dissipated, and the black depression lifted. Patrick could eat and hold down food again.

After several uneventful days, Patrick convinced himself that he had overreacted. He must have been hit by a stomach flu that affected his thinking. Spirits don't live in statues—that was ridiculous!

He gazed out at the statue. Its face was fluid. Now it appeared to be scowling, as though it did not appreciate being left outside. Patrick brought it back in and restored it to its location by the sliding glass door.

Within hours, Patrick was ill with nausea, and a terrible stench filled the house. When he touched the statue, the electrical charge went through him again.

Patrick wasted no time setting the statue outside again. He pondered what to do with it. The weird man now seemed evil. Should he destroy it? Put it out with the trash? Take it back to the flea market? He was seized by an irrational but terrifying thought: What if he could not get rid of it? What if the statue came back, like those demonic haunted dolls in horror movies?

Patrick did not know who to consult or where to turn for help. A search led him to John.

After hearing the details, John explained to Patrick how objects can acquire spirit attachments. The statue probably housed an unhappy spirit. "You did the right thing to put it outside," John said, "but when you brought it back in, you gave the spirit permission to do whatever it wanted."

"I don't understand," Patrick said. "How does a wooden statue become attached? And by what, exactly?"

"There are several possibilities," said John. "Sometimes spirits of former owners become attached to things they liked, and the spirits can react negatively to a new owner. Some objects become haunted because previous owners experimented in magic, and attracted a spirit that stayed. Some objects hold emotional residues from owners that take on a personality."

"You know, I had the impression that the man who sold it to me was glad to get rid of it," Patrick remembered.

"He may have experienced activity like you did," said John, "and he got rid of the activity by passing the statue on to a new owner—you."

"I'll destroy it," Patrick stated emphatically.

"No, that could make things worse," John warned. "The spirit probably would jump into something else. I know how to take care of it."

Later that day, John removed the weird man from Patrick's patio. He performed a cleansing and bound the spirit to the object. It was a low level, trouble-making spirit that somehow had found a home in the statue, and acted out against whoever came into possession of it. By binding the spirit to the object, it would be unable to roam about and cause paranormal activity.

Patrick was relieved of all symptoms. "I don't ever want to see that thing again," he told John. "You can have it!"

The weird man joined John's Museum of the Paranormal. Even though it is now inert, visitors to the museum swear they see the man's expression change, as though it is contemplating its next move. Look at the weird man, look away, and then look back—the face is different. And never friendly.

A visitor dubbed the figure "Mr. Sinister" and the name stuck. Perhaps the spirit bound to the statue is waiting for an opportunity to break free again.

As long as the statue resides under John's watchful care, Mr. Sinister will have a very long wait.

Not every case of paranormal activity has a clear explanation. We will never know exactly how the statue acquired a spectral occupant, and how many owners were affected by it.

As we have pointed out, not every old object found second hand in a flea market or estate shop or online comes with a paranormal track record. The moral of this story is, pay attention to your intuition and gut instinct. If you handle something and it gives you a strange feeling or sense of dread, it is a genuine warning, not your imagination.

10

The Jester Had the Last Laugh

Lately Sophia had noticed a change in her friend, Martina. Normally the light of every party and the center of every attention, Martina had been subdued and quiet. She was withdrawn at the botanica where they both worked, as though she were preoccupied. Sophia watched her pick out candles, herbs, and oils for herself, wondering what she was doing at night at home. There seemed to be a lot of spell casting going on.

"Do you have a new client?" Sophia asked one day, dying for information but not wanting to pry. Martina was reputed to be highly skilled in Santerian magic, an art that Sophia wanted to learn.

Martina gave her a sly look out of the corners of her eyes. "A new client? You could say that," she said. She gave no more information.

Sophia let it go, but she made careful mental notes of the things she saw Martina buying. Someone was having love trouble.

Maybe it was Martina who needed romantic help. Sophia knew that five years had passed since Martina's divorce, and she had not been in a steady relationship for a long time. Sophia thought of her own husband, Emilio, and their two daughters, both in their pre-teens. They made a good family, the four of them, and she was grateful for her blessings. Emilio had been distracted in recent weeks, but Sophia chalked it up to the demands of his contracting business. He was sometimes deeply absorbed and spent long hours on the job.

Sophia wondered why Martina had not done successful love spells for herself. Martina learned her craft from her mother and grandmother, and surely knew how to do it. Sophia had asked Martina for tutoring several times, but Martina always demurred, saying she was too busy with clients after working hours.

At closing time, Sophia selected some things to replenish her home supplies. It was a good time for another house cleansing, and she was low on Florida water and Reckitt's Blue Squares for floor washes. She added a few colored candles to her basket, then checked out and headed to her car. Martina was already gone, having not said good-bye.

A light snow was falling, and Sophia had to clean off the windows and windshield. Christmas was only two weeks away, and she still had a great deal of gift shopping to do. She wondered what Emilio would give her this year. He always delighted in surprising her with something extravagant.

The demands of the approaching holidays took up Sophia's attention, and she put off doing the cleansing. It could wait until after the new year.

She had no idea that by then it would be too late.

The last present under the Christmas tree was a large box wrapped in foil paper covered with green and red diamond shapes and tied with wide red ribbon. "It's for you," Emilio said to Sophia as he pulled it out from under low branches.

"Oh!" said Sophia, pulling her gaze away from the giant, sparkling diamond ring on her finger, Emilio's present to her.

"It's not from me," he said, smiling.

"Who is it from? What is it?" demanded daughters Olivia and Paula, almost in unison. "Open it, mama!"

Sophia took the box and balanced it on her lap. It was not heavy. She looked at the tag. "It's from Martina!" she exclaimed. How odd—she and Martina had never gotten into the habit of exchanging gifts on any occasion. Immediately, Sophia felt badly, for she had not given Martina a present.

She looked at Emilio, puzzled.

"She brought it to me at the office," he said with a shrug. "She wanted to surprise you and wanted me to sneak it into the house."

Sophia was still puzzled. Why a present, and why go to such lengths to keep it a secret, instead of giving it to Sophia directly? She had no time to think it through.

"Hurry up, mama," insisted Olivia. "Let's see what it is!"

"Yes, yes," replied Olivia. She tore away the wrapping. Inside the plain box, beneath wads of tissue paper, was a doll. She pulled it out and held it up.

It was a jester doll, dressed in a green and red diamond costume similar to the colors of the wrapping paper. His jester cap hung in three points ending in little bells, and his pointed slippers also ended in bells at the toes. He held a wand with a star on the top in one hand. His face was long with a hooked chin and a silly grin.

"How curious," said Sophia, not knowing how to react. She was not a doll collector, and she and Martina had never talked about dolls, other than magical poppets. It was a very strange present.

Emilio widened his eyes and pursed his lips as if to say, *Don't ask me!*

"Why did Martina give you that?" said Paula. "It's crazy."

"I don't know," Sophia answered. "It's very nice and it was very thoughtful of her." She turned the doll over in her hands. "It's made well." Her face brightened. "He looks Christmas-y, doesn't he?" She propped the doll beneath the tree. "There. Jester has a home."

At work after Christmas, Sophia thanked Martina for the doll. "It was so unexpected," she said. "I'm sorry I don't—"

Martina dismissed her with a wave of her hand. "Please, do not apologize. I saw the doll in a store and he was so cute. It was an impulse. Where did you put him?"

"Right now he is sitting under the tree," said Sophia. "I will find a spot for him when we take the tree down."

"Good, very good." Martina made another one of her sly smiles and went off to help a customer who had just entered the botanica.

There was a marked shift in the atmosphere at home after Christmas. Sophia felt it the most when she got up in the morning, and when she came home from work. At first, she thought it was just the inevitable letdown from the excitement of Christmas, but the somber air did not lift. After New Year's Day, the tree came down, and the air was still heavy.

The jester went to a new perch, seated by the hearth in the family room. Sophia was not certain she liked the doll. She felt she had to like it, since it was a present from Martina, but in truth she thought the doll was scary. Jesters always looked like they were about to play a bad joke on you.

Adding to the black clouds was new tension between Sophia and Emilio. They had frequent arguments, far more than usual, and Emilio seemed out of sorts almost all the time. He spent more hours away from home. Sophia started resenting his long absences. She hadn't minded before, but now she felt Emilio neglected her and the girls.

"So nice of you to spend some time at home," she snapped once when he came home late.

Emilio ignored her and headed to the bedroom.

"That's right, don't talk to me," shouted Sophia, trailing after him. Within seconds they were engaged in a screaming match.

"If you don't like it here, then get out," Sophia said.

"I think I will," said Emilio. He grabbed his jacket and stormed out the door.

Emilio did not come home that night.

Then a new wave of strangeness set in: household objects broke at an alarming rate. Glasses, dishes, cups, anything breakable slipped out of Sophia's hands and crashed to the floor. Vases and kitchen items on counters somehow flew off and smashed. Sophia wept when one of her favorite possessions, a figurine inherited from her grandmother, fell and shattered into tiny pieces.

It can't be me, she thought. *I can't possibly be this clumsy.*

Tapping and banging sounds were heard in the night, coming from the walls. Sophia started catching glimpses of dark, shadowy figures zipping through the house.

As the activity escalated, Sophia spent more and more time in prayer. She must have committed a sin to be punished in this way. Maybe she was being too hard on Emilio. A devout Catholic, she prayed to Mary, Jesus, God, the angels, saints, and even her ancestors. She also prayed to the *orishas*, the Santerian gods and goddesses, whose personalities overlapped with Christian saints. She prepared a floor wash for cleansing the house and lit candles.

Nothing made a dent in the heavy atmosphere or the paranormal activity.

One morning Sophia awakened with her arms sore. She was shocked to see her forearms marked with long red gouges, as though she had been raked with a nail. Her lower legs were peppered with ugly bruises. Even more shocking was the appearance of a curved red bruise that looked like a bite mark.

She showed the marks to Emilio, whose reaction astonished her. "Why are you doing this to yourself?" he said. "So you can try to accuse me of beating you?"

Sophia was stunned that Emilio would even think she would mutilate herself as a way of attacking him. Another argument ensued.

The physical damage galvanized Sophia to action. Only evil spirits could do something like this. She called her priest and asked to see him.

The priest listened patiently as she described the deterioration of her household and marriage. "Evil spirits have invaded my home," Sophia said. "I do not know why and I swear I have done nothing to justify this. I have tried to send them away and I cannot."

"How about your husband?" asked the priest. "Do you think he is the cause?"

"We have our problems as I have told you, Father," said Sophia, "but I know nothing. Maybe he is involved in a bad business deal…" She left the speculation unfinished.

The priest agreed to visit her at home and perform a house blessing.

Sophia felt profoundly relieved as she left the church. The father would set everything right again.

At the botanica, Sophia confided to Martina what was going on. In spite of her elation at anticipating the priest's solution, she could not ignore the odd expression on Martina's face. It reminded her of a cat. You look a cat in the face, and you never know what it is thinking.

Sophia could not wait for the priest to arrive to bless the house. She counted the hours and minutes. When he was done blessing every room, Sophia was convinced that a peace settled over the atmosphere. She felt as though she had been holding her breath for weeks, and now she could let go and relax.

The peace was short-lived. That night, the wall banging started again, and now it was thunderous. Sophia felt like she was being attacked by dozens of invisible mosquitoes that made sharp pricks on her. The black forms returned, bolder than before, lingering when she saw them instead of disappearing.

Even Emilio was annoyed by the phenomena, and, strangely, he was upset that Sophia had called the priest. "We don't need people thinking we're crazy," he said. "Demons! You're mind has been twisted by that botanica. I told you not to take that job, to find a normal job." He accused Sophia of engineering the trouble. They fought bitterly and Emilio left again. The girls stayed in their rooms, upset by the quarreling and frightened that the house was under siege by supernatural evil.

In the morning, Sophia felt drained and exhausted. She noticed fresh bruises on her arms and legs. She was sore all over, as though she had been beaten. She called the botanica and said she was taking a sick day.

Sophia was straightening up the bedroom when she made a horrible discovery: evidence that Emilio was having an affair. She found credit card receipts for meals at expensive restaurants, places she had not been to with Emilio, and a damning receipt for women's lingerie that Sophia had never received.

Sophia had always respected her husband's privacy and never went through his papers or belongings, but now she was compelled to do so. She made a careful search of the bedroom and Emilio's study, and found more evidence that an affair had been going on for some time. What stung even more was the fact that he had been careless about the evidence, as though he wanted her to know.

She gathered all the receipts and evidence together, dumped them in a pile on the kitchen table, and waited for Emilio to come home. She told the girls to visit their friends after school, and gave them permission to stay overnight.

For a change, Emilio came home at his usual time. He took one glance at the receipts and papers on the table and his face hardened.

Sophia flew at him in a rage. Stone-faced, he let her scream until her energy ran out.

Finally Emilio spoke. "Yes, it's true."

"Why *why?*" sobbed Sophia, tears streaming down her face. "How could you do this to me—to your family? Who is it? Tell me, tell me!"

Emilio's jaw muscles twitched. "It is Martina."

Sophia was stunned. "Martina? Martina at the botanica?"

Emilio nodded.

Sophia felt as though she had been hit by a tractor trailer. She sank onto a kitchen chair and put her head down on the table, sobbing. *Betrayed! Betrayed on all fronts!*

Emilio told her coldly that he did not want a divorce, or a separation—but he did not intend to give up Martina. He seemed like another man, someone Sophia did not know.

Sophia cried herself to sleep alone that night. When every last bit of emotion was wrung out of her, she knew she had to take matters into her own hands.

At the botanica, Sophia pulled Martina into the back room and confronted her about the affair. She was cool and under control—no screaming as with Emilio.

Sophia called Martina a few appropriate names and said, "Leave my husband alone. Go find a man of your own."

Martina looked haughty, not the least embarrassed or remorseful. "It's not going to work that way, Sophia," she said. "I have loved Emilio for a long time, from the first time I saw him when he came into the store that one day. He looked at me and our eyes met, and I knew we were destined to be together. We were meant for each other. No, Sophia, it's not me who should leave—you leave."

"I am not going anywhere. I am Emilio's wife, and he is the father of our children!"

"You have lost him, and there is nothing you can do about it," said Martina. "The *orishas* are on my side. I might as well tell you, there is a curse upon your marriage and your house. I put the curse on you, carried in by that jester I gave you—the jester that Emilio brought into the house himself. I will get everything you have, your husband, your house, your money—everything!" Martina laughed. "You were so blind."

Sophia did not know what to say. "I—I will destroy that doll," she sputtered. "I will send the curse back on you and more."

Martina laughed again. "You can't do that," she said. "There is no way to break the curse. I will win. I have won already."

With that, a physical fight of punching, hair pulling, and screaming erupted, and had to be broken up by the botanica manager. He sent both of them home and told them not to come back if they could not behave. "Settle your score somewhere else," he said. "Not here."

Sophia had no idea what to do. She went into total shock and black despair. She could not believe how her world had been shattered.

Her next confrontation was with Emilio. But when Sophia told him about Martina's curse and that he too was under a spell, he laughed. "You expect me to believe that?" he said. "I do what I want—nobody makes me do anything."

Sophia's life continued to deteriorate. The house remained full of black figures and paranormal activity, and empty of her husband. She sent the girls away to stay with a relative for a while. She did not know what to do with the doll. She was afraid to destroy it or throw it away, but she didn't want it in the house, either. She put it in a box and placed it in the trunk of her car. At least it was out of sight.

She refused to surrender. There had to be a solution, someone who could help her. She spent hours at the computer, searching the internet for ideas. There were many sites that offered magical remedies, but Sophia felt that would only make matters worse. She didn't know enough about such matters herself, and Martina was skilled. What if she could detect counter magic and then increase her own attack?

Then Sophia found John's website. She liked what she read and called his number.

John was alarmed when he heard the full story from Sophia. Curses could be extremely hard to break, and this one was deeply embedded in a severe case. He was glad to hear that Sophia had not done anything to the jester doll. An object imbued with a curse carries one or more attached demonic spirits tasked with carrying out the curse. Destroying their home or carrier object can cause the spirits to jump ship to something else, potentially compounding the problem. In this case, so much time had elapsed that the demonic entities might already have migrated into the environment.

John kept these concerns to himself as he talked with Sophia, not wanting to add to her upset. "Keep up your prayers," he said. "Let me handle the doll."

The situation at Sophia's home was indeed grave. Within minutes of his arrival, John was tapped on the head by invisible fingers. This was one of the personal signs that always indicated the presence of a strong demonic entity. Martina evidently had been able to summon up a heavy force. After the head tapping came the sensation of being grabbed and bear-hugged from behind. This was a brazen entity.

John summoned up his own protective measures and pushed the presence away. Sophia had taken the doll out of her car trunk and brought it into the house for John. He treated the doll with holy water, sea salt, and prayer, and then did a cleansing with holy water and sea salt throughout the house. In response, banging sounded on the walls and then gradually subsided.

He told Sophia the doll should be removed from the property.

"Please take it," she said. "Get rid of it. What will happen now to the curse?"

"Usually removing the host object ends the activity," said John. "But I have to warn you, sometimes it makes things worse. Then we have to come back again."

"Is it true that a curse goes back on the person who sends it? Will this go back on Martina?"

"Dark magic always has consequences," John said. "Practitioners think they can stay one step ahead and outsmart everyone, including the spirits they summon. There is always a price to pay, and Martina will pay hers. It may not happen as fast as you want, but you have to let spiritual justice take its course."

Sophia nodded solemnly. "I just want my husband back and my home to be unbroken."

"Let's take one step at a time," said John.

On his way home, John's car engine died inexplicably—another sign of a powerful entity. He coasted to the side of the road, then treated the jester again and invoked spiritual protection. The engine started up, and he was able to make it home without further incident. The jester remained outside while John performed more cleansing and a binding.

John's worries about the severity of the situation were soon realized. The removal of the jester caused a marked increase in paranormal activity, indicating that a serious infestation had lodged in Sophia's house.

Sophia's voice was strained when she called John to report the increase. "Everything is worse," she cried. "How is this helping? What am I going to do?"

"I know it may not seem like it, but we've made progress," John reassured her. "I told you this could happen. The entity has come up against resistance and it is fighting back, still trying to carry out the curse. We have to repeat a blessing." He recommended that she have her priest come back.

Sophia appealed to her priest, who returned and performed another blessing. As he intoned his prayers and admonitions, the pressure in the house escalated, and the banging increased. Then the dark force weakened, and broke.

The atmosphere cleared like the sky after a hurricane has passed. Just like a physical hurricane, this hurricane from hell left wreckage behind.

"There is still a lot of work left to be done," John told Sophia on their next consultation. "Martina's magical influence is broken, but you and your husband have to fix your marriage. If you don't, the curse still wins from the damage that was done."

Once the curse was broken, Emilio was suddenly disinterested in Martina, and offered no explanation why. He continued to deny that there had been any curse. Martina, of course, had never told him what she had done, as she wanted him to believe that he wanted her out of his own desire. It took Sophia and Emilio a lot of time and a great deal of effort, but they reconciled their marriage.

The friendship between Sophia and Martina was destroyed, and neither could stand being in the presence of the other. In the past, Sophia had always subordinated herself to Martina, who had a stronger and more forceful personality, but now she had found new spiritual strength. She resolved not to quit her job at the botanica in order to avoid Martina, but would make her presence Martina's problem. Within a few weeks, Martina was gone. One day she did not show up for work. Sophia learned that she had quit without notice.

The jester still has a smirk, despite being rendered harmless as a host for a curse-wielding demonic spirit. In a battle for control, someone always loses. The woman who lost this battle for illicit love had intended to be the winner. The woman who won the battle suffered an emotional scar that would be with her the rest of her life.

The only one who had the last laugh was the jester.

Attempting to control people with magical spells and curses never works in the long run. Limited success might be achieved at first, but ultimately people cannot be commanded like drones. Martina got carried away by her own blindness and put herself and others at great risk.

Another scenario might have played out from the tragic case if the balance of power had shifted the other way and Martina had succeeded in prying Emilio away from his wife and family. For a time, everything would have seemed perfect. Maintaining the hold on Emilio would have required tremendous amounts of ongoing effort and energy, however, and at some point Martina would have exhausted her own resources. Dark entities feed off the life force of humans, including those who summon them—it is one form of payment in exchange for their services. A demonic spirit would have vampirized Martina until she was a shell. At that point, Emilio would have become disenchanted, perhaps even remorseful, and would have left Martina. Could he have repaired his marriage? Maybe, maybe not. Either way, lives would have been ruined.

Thanks to Sophia's timely appeal to John, she was set on the right course. We do not know what happened to Martina. There is always a price when it comes to trafficking with spirits, and Martina had to pay hers.

11

Spirit in the Mask

You've heard the adage, "Don't play with matches—you might get burned." There is another adage of equal importance: "Don't play with masks—you might get possessed."

We are not talking about the play masks that people wear to costume parties and children wear at Halloween, or the ethnic masks made commercially to sell to the tourist trade. We are referring to real masks, ritually made by hand to house gods and spirits, and to merge the human wearer with those beings. Those masks were never intended to be decorations or playthings, as one New England physician discovered.

On a trip to England, Lynne made a special point of visiting as many antique shops as possible, looking for treasures that would be hard to find in the States: art, sterling silver serving and decorative pieces, antique maps, and the like. In one London shop, she became entranced by a large wooden mask. It looked African, and though the shopkeeper concurred, he could not add any more detail. The mask had come from the estate of a collector who traveled. That was all he knew.

Lynne was not looking for masks on this trip, but this one captivated her. The shopkeeper showed her other tribal objects that had come from the same estate. She purchased the mask and several of the items, and arranged to have them shipped home. She had a few other masks from other cultures, so this would make a fine expansion of the collection.

The mask had an otherworldly air about it, more so than any other mask she had purchased. It was oval shaped and carved of dark wood that had been smoothly polished. The forehead had a peculiar, high dome that jutted out, and the top of the head was covered in thick braids made of tan-colored twine. A small bundle of bits of stone and perhaps bones, wrapped in thin twine, sat atop the head. The heavy lips were open. Most riveting of all were the eyes, which were two round holes the size of quarters. Their black depths seemed to gaze out into another realm. The face looked almost corpse-like.

When the items arrived, Lynne installed the mask on a wall where she entertained guests, and placed the other objects around the home. She was sure to get admiring comments on the mask. Her wealth enabled to her have fine collections of prizes from all over the world, and she enjoyed displaying them.

Soon after the arrival of the mask, a change came over Lynne and her showplace house. She caught glimpses of dark, shadowy forms flitting about. She saw them out of the corners of her eyes, but when she looked directly, they would be gone. Sometimes when she was moving about the house, she saw a shadow form dart across a room or hallway and then vanish.

She dismissed them as imagination, plays of light and natural shadow, and fatigue. She hadn't seen the moving shadows before, or had a history of seeing shadows, but in the back of her mind, she knew there had to be a rational explanation. Lynne was a doctor, and for her, science explained everything. There was no such reality as the supernatural, so thoughts of spirits and ghosts never entered her head.

Then a strange, repetitive pattern of dreams set in. The dreams were distinctly different than most of her other dreams. Lynne did not pay much attention to dreams in general, as she considered them to be chemical reactions in the brain tied to the release of stress.

These weird dreams kept repeating. They were intensely realistic, as though Lynne were awake in a peculiar reality and a strange place. The air looked heavy, almost touchable. She could see and hear and touch with remarkable clarity.

In the dreams, she suddenly found herself out in a field or plain of tall grass. The sun beat down with great intensity, and the air was humid. The dirt below her bare feet was hard. She was with other people, who were black and wearing tribal garb of some sort. Everyone, including her, seemed to be involved in a ritual, moving and dancing and chanting with great energy to the beat of rapid drumming. She could not understand the chants. She could not see herself, but she could feel herself participating. In the background, shadowy forms moved to and fro.

She always felt disoriented upon awakening, as though she had been to a real place, and now her "other" place, home, seemed alien to her.

When the dreams did not stop after a few nights, Lynne worried that something was wrong with her. Were these signs of a mental breakdown?

One night she was jolted out of the dream by a weight that came down on her bed, as though a large person had sat down forcefully upon it. Lynne gasped and sat up, wide awake. She was alone in the bed. As her eyes adjusted to the darkness, she saw that she was also alone in the room. There was no one on the bed. She cautiously waved her hand over the space where she thought the weight had settled.

Did she imagine it? Was it part of the dream? Trying to rationalize it away did not help, and Lynne could not sleep the rest of the night.

She arose in the early morning hours, only to see the shadow forms flitting about.

That was the last straw.

Lynne arrived for work at her clinic feeling stressed and distracted. She could not function this way. Something was wrong, and whatever it was, she had to fix it. She reached for her phone and dialed a physician she knew, and booked an appointment.

Lynne underwent a battery of tests and then waited impatiently for days for the results. Meanwhile, she endured the drumming, chanting, and dancing dreams nightly.

Nothing organically wrong could be identified. Physically, Lynne was in good health, the doctor said. Her colleague suggested that maybe she just needed a vacation for complete rest, and gave her a prescription for sedatives.

The pills did not help to ease her mounting anxiety, nor did they put an end to the strange nocturnal activity.

Lynne's next recourse was a psychiatrist, but he could find no signs of mental breakdown. Convinced she was indeed having one, Lynne consulted another psychiatrist, only to be told the same diagnosis.

Lynne's failure to find a rational reason for the phenomena was nearly as upsetting as the phenomena. When a friend suggested a supernatural cause, Lynne bristled. "You don't expect me to believe in such ridiculous nonsense, do you?" she said. "Please!"

One night she was surfing the internet in hopes of finding something that would help her solve her dilemma. To her dismay, everything that matched her description of the activity pointed to a supernatural or paranormal website.

Maybe… just maybe… she would take a peek. If she found lurid websites festooned with flaming skulls, demons and jumping devils, then that would be the end of it. She regarded people involved in the occult and paranormal as "fringe people" operating under fantasy and delusion. What they needed was a good dose of science!

Lynne was about confront a painful truth: the supernatural world exists, is real, and affects people of all stations, backgrounds, education, and mindsets. It does not discriminate. And science comes up empty-handed for most it.

Fortunately for Lynne, she hit the jackpot on her first try: John's Paranormal Research Society of New England website. She spent some time on the pages. The whole concept of the paranormal was foreign to her, but at least there was nothing here to send her running. There was even a phone number listed on the contact information. That was gutsy. She wondered how many nut case calls were made to the website's owner, John Zaffis. He looked normal—no weird clothes or occult jewelry. "The Godfather of the Paranormal." He must have some experience under his belt.

She picked up the phone and punched in the number.

Fortunately again for Lynne, it was one of the rare nights when John was home, and not out on the road or on a case.

"This is Lynne _____, and I'm a medical doctor," Lynne began. "I feel rather foolish calling you and I hope you don't think I'm nuts, but…" She described what had been happening to her.

"What you've described is more common than you might think," said John.

"Really? I'm very uncomfortable," said Lynne. "Do you mind if I ask you some questions?"

"Not a bit," said John.

Lynne asked John about his background, what sort of cases he had, and what he did on those cases. She was full of stereotyped impressions about the paranormal, and wanted to make certain that there wasn't going to be any dark magic involved by people wearing black robes. As they talked, she found John to be pleasant, personable, and to have a great sense of humor.

Then it was John's turn to ask questions. Had she moved? Was there anyone in the house who was involved in the occult? Did she have any relationship problems? Had she had any major changes in life or health? Had she brought anything into the house right before the activity started, especially second hand?

She answered no to all but the last question. "I was in England recently and came home with a few things. I have some collections."

"Tell me exactly what you brought home," he said.

When Lynne got to the mask, John stopped her and asked for a description and more details about how and where she had acquired it.

"That's your problem, right there," he said when she was done.

"The mask?"

"Tribal masks are not made for decoration," said John. "Yes, there are masks made for tourists, but the real ones are made for a ritual purpose, and to become the houses for a deity or spirit. This mask probably has a deity or spirit attached to it that came into your home, and now it's creating activity."

Lynne was shocked into silence. Then she managed, "That's preposterous!"

"If you do some research on masks, you'll find plenty to back up what I'm saying," John replied.

"But it wasn't doing anything in the shop!"

"We don't know that for certain," John said.

Lynne was still flabbergasted and for a split second thought about hanging up.

She decided to stay on the line. "You mean to tell me that some spirit lives in the mask and is responsible for the shadow figures and my dreams?"

"Yes, and also that feeling you had of a weight on the bed. Like I was saying, what you've described is more common than you might think. There may not be a mask involved, but in such cases as yours there is an object with a spirit attached to it."

"Spirits can cause dreams?"

"I know this is new to you," John answered. "Under certain conditions, they can influence a person's dreams. The dreams you've been having probably are scenes from the native land where the mask was made. There would have been dancing, chanting and drumming during rituals."

"I'm a doctor," Lynne reminded John. "Science says that—"

"You won't find any of this in science books," said John. "But it *is* in your home. Do you want to do something about it?"

"Can't I just ignore it? Will it go away?"

"Probably not, and there's a good chance that it will get worse," said John. "The spirit wants to go home, or at least have the mask used for its original purpose."

Lynne was silent once again. When she spoke, her voice was harsh. "Well, just how do I get rid of this god or spirit?"

"If you want to get rid of the activity, take the mask out of the house. The spirit will not go away—it will still be attached to the mask—but at least it won't be in your home. I can also come over and do a binding on it." He explained what a binding was, and that it would keep the spirit quiet.

Lynne agreed to have John come over. "I don't want to keep the mask," she said. "Do whatever you have to do and take it away." She arranged an appointment and ended the call.

Lynne was in a state of agitation. Her entire worldview had been struck by lightning.

She went to the mask, still hanging on the wall, and gazed at it. Where once it had seemed exotic, it now seemed terrifying. The round, bottomless black eye holes stared out into deep space. Before, it was a piece of carved and polished wood. Now, it was *alive.* Lynne suddenly saw it in a completely new light. And she did not like it.

Before the scheduled appointment, John received another call from Lynne. She sounded on the verge of hysteria. "I'm still having the dreams and seeing those black shadows," she said. "I am at my wit's end! I don't know what to do! I am so creeped out I don't even want *you* in the

house. I'm putting the mask out by the front door. Just come by and get it!"
The call ended with a click.

John tried calling her back, but the call went to voicemail.

Lynne was not the first person by a long shot to freak out and
dump a haunted object as fast as possible. Nor was she the first one to be
in denial about the supernatural. There was only so much John could do. If
victims chose not to believe, that was their choice.

When John arrived at the house, he saw a box sitting on the front
porch. Yes, that was it—the mask was inside. He did not ring the bell, just
took the mask and left.

The mask was bound and added to the Museum of the Paranormal.

John let a few days go by and then phoned Lynne to see how she
was doing.

She sounded weary. "The dreams have stopped, but the shadow
forms are still here, and sometimes I hear knocking noises."

"It might be the other ritual objects you bought with the mask,"
John said.

"Yes, and they're all going to the auction house," said Lynne. "In
fact, I'm getting rid of the other masks I have. I'm not going to collect them
anymore."

"There's no harm in collecting as long as you know what some of
the issues are," said John.

"I'm not taking chances. This has been quite difficult for me. I've
had to do some serious reevaluation, because clearly, there are things that
science cannot explain. I don't like thinking about it, and I don't like talking
about it, either."

John asked if there was anything else he could do for her.

"Not right now," she said. "I'll let you know if so."

John never heard from Lynne again. Presumably, the removal of all
objects from the house eliminated the remaining activity. One thing was
certain: Lynne would never collect another mask, no matter how innocent
it looked.

Sometimes the skeptical retreat into their cocoons of denial and
disbelief. If they are lucky, they never have to deal with a paranormal
problem again. Sometimes the first run-in opens the door to at least the
possibility of other encounters. Those who are not in denial are much
better prepared the next time around.

When Rosemary saw the mask, she recognized telltale features about it, including the round eye sockets, the braided hair, the domed forehead, and the large open lips. "This probably came from the Ivory Coast region of Africa," she told John. "Their masks are famous. I'll see what I can find out."

The mask had the features of ritual masks made by the Dan people, who have occupied the Ivory Coast and Liberia region of western Africa since about the eighth century BC. The Dan have had the reputation of being fierce warriors.

Traditionally, they define two realms: the human realm, which comprises their village, and the sacred spirit realm, which comprises the forest. The forest is the domain of spirits and wild animals. One crossed from the human realm to the spirit realm by saying certain prayers and wearing items from both realms. A mask, made of wood from the spirit realm, forms the ideal bridge. It embodies and represents a spirit, who can manifest through the mask without risk of injury to mere mortals.

The trees used for masks are inhabited by spirits, and so before a tree is cut down, a sacrifice is made to the spirit and permission to cut it is asked.

The mask makers have learned their art from family elders or as apprentices to a craftsman. New masks might be inspired by dreams, which are presented to elders who determine if the mask should be made.

The mask is carved with an adze, a curved knife, which also houses its own spirit. The tool is passed down through generations.

There are variations in style; in general, there are "female" masks and "male" masks. Lynne had acquired a male mask, with round eyes and a full face. Female masks are oval and pointed, with slender, slanted eye sockets.

A mask has its own dancer—always male—for rituals. Wearing the mask transforms the dancer into the spirit who resides in the mask. The spirit speaks through the dancer in its own language, which cannot be understood. Certain elders can understand the language and translate it.

Similar beliefs about masks and procedures for making them exist around the world.

Real masks do find their way into the hands of collectors. The spirits they house often are not happy to be taken out of their native land and turned into something taboo, a mere house decoration. In a new and strange environment, they get loose and create activity.

If such an object cannot be returned to its homeland, it is possible, during the binding, to help a dislocated spirit find its way back home. In some cases, the spirit remains with the object and goes into dormancy.

We usually think of masks as hiding or disguising identity, but the true nature of masks is to reveal something hidden. The next time you wear a mask—even a costume mask—ask yourself: What are you revealing and releasing into the world?

12

The Squishy Faces

The bookends were ugly as sin, but Jared felt obliged to keep them. He pulled all of the packing paper off and looked around for a place to put them. There was an open space on the bookshelf in the living room. Perfect.

Jared's new wife, Crystal, came in while he was unpacking. Their marriage was barely a few weeks old, and their elegant new house was strewn with packing boxes.

"How's it going?" Crystal asked with a smile.

Jared shrugged, a bit of guilt passing through him. "It's going," he answered, pawing through the paper.

Crystal peered into the box. "What are those things?" She pointed to a collection of small objects that were partially out of the packing paper.

"Nothing, just some stuff from Marla."

Crystal frowned. "You still have some of *her* things? Why?"

Jared shrugged again. "I guess I forgot I had them."

"Forgot? How could you forget? They've been packed! *I* didn't pack them."

Jared made aimless motions with his hands.

"I don't want them here," Crystal said firmly. "You know how I feel about her. Get rid of them—give them back to her."

"They were presents," Jared protested. "You don't give back presents."

"Then throw them out. I don't have any reminders around of my old relationships," Crystal retorted. Her eyes lighted upon the bookshelf. "What in God's name are those ugly things?"

Jared went to the shelf. "Bookends. Marla made them. She gave them to me after we broke up, and said she didn't want any hard feelings between us."

Crystal examined them. They were indeed hideous: slabs with blobs of faces that were distorted, as though they had melted in the sun. The faces were wrapped in kerchiefs. They had hostile eyes and thick, blubbery lips that were parted in scowls. They were crudely painted and fired in a dark gray color.

"They look like a couple of squishy faces," she said, her voice full of disapproval. "And cheap, too. We can afford whatever we want—these are trash."

Jared felt obliged to rise to his former lover's defense. "They were a peace offering," he said, irritated. "I don't see any harm in keeping them."

Crystal's face flushed. "What hold does she still have on you? You said it was over. You're married to me now!"

Jared met her icy gaze. "Leave it alone, Crystal. They're not going to do any harm."

Jared had no idea that exactly the opposite would soon be the case.

The relationship between Jared and Marla had always been turbulent. When they met, Jared found Marla to be mysterious and exotic. She was interested in the occult and knew a great deal about magic, rituals, the paranormal, and all sorts of strange topics. Marla was headstrong and domineering, but possessed an allure that Jared could not resist. He often joked that Marla had bewitched him, and she always laughed, her dark eyes pools of unknown depth.

Over time, the relationship proved to be exhausting. Jared was always catering to Marla. Whenever she was displeased, she turned nasty and manipulative. If provoked, she could fly into a fury that would astonish the gods. She had a secret side to her, and Jared had the impression that she led a secret life to which he was not privy.

Marla made it clear that she wanted to marry Jared, but he put her off. He wasn't certain he was ready to marry anyone, even Marla.

Then he met Crystal at a business function. He was immediately captivated by her, but in a much different way. She was everything he wanted in a lifetime partner. They hit it off right away, and he started seeing more and more of her.

But Jared could not pull himself away from Marla. Crystal knew that he was seeing another woman, who he said was more of a friend than a serious romantic interest. It wasn't quite true, but Jared felt he needed the right moment to let go. As the relationship between Jared and Crystal progressed, Crystal was not happy that he hung on to Marla, but she put on a patient front.

Then Marla found out about Crystal. Jared could never figure out how—it was as though she read his thoughts or saw into his heart. Marla confronted him and he admitted that he was involved with Crystal, and that it was serious. In fact, he wanted to marry Crystal.

Marla went into a rage. "How dare you!" she screamed, launching into a tirade against him. "I guarantee you that you will never, ever be happy with her! And you will never be successful at anything you do!"

The intensity of her rage was so extreme that her words shook Jared to his core. He felt as though they stabbed deep into him.

Soon after the blow-up, Jared proposed to Crystal, and she accepted. They began planning an elaborate wedding, and the memory of Marla's fury faded. Jared confided in Crystal how the relationship had ended.

Right before the wedding, Marla contacted Jared. She was all sweetness and light. She apologized for her temper. "I don't want to end on bad feelings," she said. "I have a present for you and Crystal. Can you come over and pick it up?"

Jared was surprised, but relieved, because he, too, wanted no bad end. He was also surprised that Marla would give them a gift. It seemed more than she needed to do.

Marla greeted him at the door of her home and let him in. It was as he remembered, full of occult objects and art. Marla handed him a box wrapped in wedding paper. "I made these myself for you," she said. Her eyes glittered.

Jared opened the gift. When he saw the distorted squishy faces, he did not know what to say. They were unbelievably monstrous.

"I—I—" he stammered.

Marla smiled. "There's no need to thank me."

The squishy faces bookends stayed in their box. Jared did not show them to Crystal. He thought about disposing of them. Instead, they went into a packing box with a few personal effects of Marla's that he still had as well. Then Jason liberated them when he and Crystal moved into their new house.

The squishy faces remained on the living room bookshelf, casting their baleful gazes out into the room. Crystal made it clear that she hated them. Oddly, the more she hated them, the more determined Jared was to defend them and keep them.

The squishy faces were the only fly in the ointment, and otherwise the couple settled into building their lives together and feathering their beautiful nest. They had excellent, well-paying jobs and bright futures ahead of them. They lived in a prestigious neighborhood.

The newlywed glow lasted only about a month, and then a new energy invaded the house. It was dark and gloomy. Jared slipped into a chronic depression.

Marla returned like a bad penny, calling Jared on the telephone. At first, he talked with her briefly and politely. She was nosey, always asking how he and Crystal were getting along. Crystal was annoyed. The calls increased in frequency, even late at night.

"Marla, you really need to stop calling me," Jared finally told her. The line went dead.

The calls continued. Sometimes Marla was on the other end, asking for Jared. Sometimes there was only silence or static. Jared knew it was Marla. "Stop calling me!" he shouted into the phone even when he was greeted by silence or static. "I know it's you! Stop bothering me!"

The pestering phone calls continued.

Then Jared's email acted up. He received emails with Marla's address as sender, but the body was blank or filled with gibberish, sometimes a single letter repeated as though someone held down a repeat key. When he answered the emails, his replies bounced back as undeliverable. He blocked Marla's address, but the emails kept coming with unknown senders, just like spam. Intermixed with the gibberish emails were warnings and threats: "You are being watched," "I know what you do and where you are," and "Tell Crystal to be careful today." Some emails contained bizarre words that sounded like spells, and were accompanied by strange symbols.

Jared tried calling Marla about the emails, but her phone always went straight to voice mail. He contacted the ISP provider, but an investigation came up empty. It was as though the emails were materializing out of space straight onto his computer.

The peace in the home was destroyed, and tension mounted between Jared and his wife. Crystal could not understand why Jared did not pay a personal visit to Marla to tell her in no uncertain terms to stop harassing them. Crystal threatened to go to the police if Jared would not take action, and it was all he could do to prevent her from following through. He knew it would make matters worse. The truth was, he was frightened by Marla and what she might be capable of doing in retaliation.

Crystal began to feel watched by the squishy faces. She hated walking by their baleful glares. "I can feel their eyes on me," she told Jared. "They stare at me. They're alive!"

"That's crap," said Jared. "They're bookends, made out of clay. They can't possibly be alive."

Crystal started avoiding the living room. She spent less and less time there, and when she had to pass through the room, she sped. The squishy face eyes trailed after her, boring into her back.

Meanwhile, troubles mounted on other fronts. There were sudden financial setbacks: investments went sour and major household repairs spiked. Jared's work suffered. He would escape to the office each morning, glad to be out of the house, but at work he could not concentrate well. He lost a key account that tarnished his track record and jeopardized a promotion he hoped to land.

By the time Jared contacted John, both he and Crystal were severely frayed. Their once harmonious and happy relationship had deteriorated into bickering and quarreling.

When John paid the couple a visit, he zeroed right in on the squishy faces. The negative energy field around them was so strong, it was like a neon sign.

Jared told John about Marla. "I'm certain she was involved in witchcraft," he admitted.

"How do you know that?" John asked.

"There were a couple of times that I dropped in on her. I think I interrupted some sort of spells or rituals she was doing. She kept a lot of herbs and odd things, and she would make remarks that anyone who offended her or got on her bad side would be sorry." Jared grimaced. "I never took her seriously. I thought she was joking. She was very theatrical, you know. It never occurred to me that she would be capable of hurting me or Crystal—until lately."

"Well, buddy, you did leave her for another woman," John said gently.

"She gave me the bookends, said she made them just for me, and she didn't want any hard feelings between us," Jared protested.

"If she practiced witchcraft, she probably made them and deliberately put a spell on them for revenge," said John.

Jared shook his head. "I find that so hard to believe—how can objects cause the problems we've been having?"

"There are many ways to hex," said John. "She could have attached a spirit to them with the instructions to upset the house."

"That's why I feel watched by those ugly faces," Crystal interjected, looking at Jared. "I *told* you they were alive." She turned to John. "I just found out about Marla being a witch. Jared never told me until yesterday." She turned back to Jared. "Why did you keep that from me?"

The two started to argue. John interrupted. "Let's see what we can do to clear the air here. It will require more than taking the objects out, because your old girlfriend has been able to throw a curse."

"What about those other things of Marla's that you still have?" Crystal said.

Jared described to John the personal effects of Marla's that he had in a box. He got them out for John to examine. They felt inactive, but John nonetheless recommended that Jared dispose of them.

John treated the squishy faces with holy water, sea salt, and prayers. He outlined a plan for carrying out an exorcism on the home and on Jared. The couple agreed. John took the squishy faces with him to finish cleansing and binding them.

In a few days, John returned with clergy, and the exorcism was performed. Jared said he felt an immediate relief, as though a great weight had been lifted from him. Crystal said the air felt lighter and clearer.

"We'll see what happens in the next couple of weeks," said John.

Jared and Crystal reported no more troubling activity. Both said they continued to feel much better. "What happens to Marla?" Jared asked. "Will she know what we've done?"

"She'll know the spell was broken," John said. "We've put a lot of spiritual protection in place around you. Don't have any direct contact with her."

Jared said he and Crystal never wanted to see the squishy faces again. "Keep them. Put them in that museum of yours," he said. He added, "I got rid of Marla's personal things, too."

"What did you do with them?"

"With any luck, they're at the bottom of Long Island Sound."

Without being told, Jared had instinctively done one of the best ways to dispose of magically affected objects: submerge them in deep or running water.

Like other victims of curses, Jared's disbelief about the supernatural and magic caused him to overlook important clues. Had he paid attention to them, he could have averted most, if not all, of the activity. Marla was involved in magic and spell casting. She had cursed Jared by screaming at him that he would never be happy or successful again. The final and most telling clue was the "gift" of handmade objects, which actually were the instruments for carrying out Marla's revenge. Jared never should have accepted them or kept them, and he should have disposed of Marla's personal belongings, as well. And, given all those circumstances, he should have sought help at the first sign of unusual activity. The longer curse energy goes on, the more it becomes deeply attached to both the victim and his or her environment.

As for curses, what is the best course of action? Some believe that a curse should be returned to the sender so that they suffer their own ill wishes. Others believe a curse should be neutralized and sent into the light, or turned over to angels.

We believe there is nothing to be gained by sending a curse back, which only perpetuates the cycle of negativity. Cursed objects should be cleansed and bound, and the curse nullified in the most appropriate way, such as exorcism or giving it to the angel realm. People who throw curses inevitably suffer the consequences, for what they send out sooner or later comes back on them. The spiritual laws always see that justice is done.

13

This Violin Doesn't Play Pretty Music

Janet could not understand why her house was suddenly so cold all the time. No matter what temperature she set on the thermostat, or how warm it was outside, a chill descended inside. It was a bone-penetrating chill, like winter in a damp climate—the kind of chill that will not go away.

Today the outside temperature was in the mid-70s, going up into the 80s, the weather service predicted. Inside Janet's house, the air felt like a meat locker, despite the humming of the basement furnace that was throwing out heat.

Even a cup of hot tea, her favorite remedy for chasing away the cool blues, did not work. Janet took another sip and set her mug down on her coffee table.

Something else was going on in the house, but right now Janet was reluctant—or perhaps too frightened—to acknowledge it, even to herself. Now, the very thought of it zipping through her mind, pulled her face to face with it.

There was a presence in the house.

Something had invaded her space. It was invisible, but she knew it was there. She felt it rushing by her in a wind colder than air in the house. It always pushed her, as though it wanted to knock her over. Whatever or whoever it was, it was unhappy and angry. Janet had been finding broken things all over the house—dishes, glasses, vases, even wooden things. At first, she thought her cat McAllister was to blame, even though she knew that McAllister could not possibly have mustered the strength to smash wooden candle holders into pieces. Bump something off a counter or shelf from time to time, yes. But the scattering of the pieces looked like the objects had been hurled with great force.

The breaking of objects had begun when Janet was absent from the house. She would come home from work and find something broken on the floor. Then the activity escalated, with the sounds of shattering glass erupting in the house when Janet was home. She never saw the breaking, but heard it, and dashed to the location of the sound to find pieces on the floor. Finally she knew for certain that McAllister played no part in what was going on, when a great shattering occurred while the cat was curled next to Janet on the sofa. At the sound of glass breaking, McAllister leaped instantly to his feet and dashed from the room.

Yes, both Janet and cat were on edge.

Thus far, no damage had been done to her precious collection of antique musical instruments. A violinist by training, Janet had always had a love of fine old instruments of all kinds. She had never become a concert performer—her career had taken another path—but she earned enough money to indulge in buying valuable pieces. She had flutes, clarinets, an oboe, a baby grand piano, old sheet music, a dulcimer, and several vintage violins. Her most prized possession was an eighteenth-century violin from Austria mounted in a shadow box and grandly displayed on one of her living room walls. Janet had found the violin in a pricey estate shop.

Janet worried about her musical collection, which was spread around the house. Broken dishes and porcelain items were bad enough, but what if she found her instruments destroyed?

She wondered if the house had become haunted. But why and by what? She had lived there for eight years, and nothing unusual had ever happened in the house. Why would a ghost suddenly take up residency?

Janet pushed the thoughts from her mind. She wasn't certain she believed in ghosts, anyway. She picked up her mug and went into the kitchen to toss the remaining tea. It was her day off, and she had a long list of chores to do. She had to pass by the violin on the way. As she walked past it, the air suddenly felt colder, and she shuddered.

The house never did warm up that day.

A mystery in the night changed her mind about ghosts and hauntings.

Janet awakened from a disturbed sleep and a nightmarish dream. When she opened her eyes, she wasn't certain whether she was awake or still dreaming. The faint sound of a violin being played drifted throughout the house. *I must have left the television on*, she thought. She had fallen asleep while watching it before going to bed.

Janet got up, turned on a light and went out into the living room. Just as she reached the darkened room, the music stopped. Her skin prickled. She flicked on a light and saw that the television set was off. So was the radio in her sound system.

That's peculiar, she thought. *I must have dreamed it.*

Janet put the light out and returned to bed. She felt something follow her down the hall, but when she turned around, nothing was there.

She slept fitfully the rest of the night.

In the morning, the house felt alien, as though it wasn't the same anymore. Janet felt out of place, an intruder in her own home, as she readied herself for work. She put the bad night behind her as the day wore on and office matters occupied her attention. She felt her normal self again by the time she turned into her driveway, thinking about relaxing with a nice glass of wine.

She opened the door and was greeted by a pall of chill air. It was as though a fog had somehow settled into the house and draped it with dampness. Janet's stomach tightened. She relaxed a bit when she could see no signs of broken objects. Perhaps whatever was going on was at last coming to an end.

She turned up the thermostat and heard the furnace come on. *Where's McAllister,* she wondered, as she headed for her bedroom. The cat usually came out to greet her when she arrived home, eager for his dinner. Her mental question was answered when she opened her closet. There was McAllister, huddled into a corner. He looked up at her with a terrified expression and bolted out. She called to McAllister, but he disappeared into another part of the house.

Janet changed into sweat pants and a hoodie. She could not shake the feeling of being watched. She tried to convince herself it was just her imagination. She did not succeed.

The kitchen was cold, even with the furnace running and heat blasting out of the vents. Janet opened a bottle of white wine and poured a generous glass. In the living room, she sat down on her sofa and turned on the television, looking for something funny and distracting to watch. McAllister eventually appeared, and hopped up to his favorite spot nestled into the arm rest opposite of where Janet sat. The house continued to feel chilly, but never mind—it wasn't anything to worry about any longer.

Janet's uneasy peace abruptly ended when McAllister suddenly sat bolt right up, his gray eyes huge. He stared off toward the dark hallway to the bedrooms.

Before Janet could react, she heard the soft sound of footsteps coming down the carpeted hallway. McAllister jumped off the couch and tore out. Janet was frozen in fear and her breath stopped. *Someone was in the house!* Her adrenalin kicked into action, and she flew off the couch as fast as the cat had done, and dashed to the front door. She yanked it open and ran outside, and kept running until she was well away from the house. Then she collapsed, out of breath.

Janet looked back at the house. No one had pursued her. No lights had come on.

She debated what to do. Call the police? Go back in? She sat shivering on the front lawn until she gained control of her breath and quivering.

She decided to go back in. It must have been her imagination. She was overreacting.

Janet gingerly pushed on the front door and it creaked back on its hinges. She peered inside. The television was still going. Everything looked normal.

Steeling herself, Janet went slowly through all the rooms in the house, turning on every light in the entire place. She even went down into basement. She went through the bathrooms and looked in the closets. McAllister was still making himself scarce, but nothing else was amiss.

Janet locked all the doors and left all the lights on. The blaze somehow made her feel more secure. She returned to the television for distraction, but could not concentrate on any program that came on.

When Janet was ready to retire for the evening, she inspected the entire house again and double-checked all the locks. She turned off some of the lights, but left the hallway light on. Its glow shone into her bedroom.

Every creak and snap in the house set her nerves on edge. Eventually, another fitful sleep came over her.

In the middle of the night, Janet awakened again to the sound of faint violin music emanating from the living room. It was the same piece she had heard the night before, a classical composition she recognized. This time, she knew it was not the television set, or the radio. She pulled the covers up over her head, thinking that if she ignored it, it would go away. The music persisted, repeating over and over.

Finally she threw off the covers and got up. Just like the night before, the music abruptly stopped as she neared the living room. Nothing electronic was on, and no one was present. When she turned to go back down the hall, she once again felt an invisible presence follow her.

This pattern of activity repeated every night. The breaking of objects stopped, only to be replaced by phenomena that were far creepier. Footsteps in the hallway. Phantom violin music. An invisible presence that followed her back to her bedroom.

She could not ignore the violin music. When it started, it continued until she got up and went into the living room. It always stopped before she got there.

Janet began to feel unsafe in the house day and night. Whatever was going on was beyond her control. She resisted talking to anyone about it—they would think her crazy.

The paranormal activity wore down Janet's emotions. She felt frayed around the edges, and jumpy. After about a week, she was ready to move out. Perhaps if she left for a while, she thought, "it" would go away.

"What do you want?" she would demand to the air, but nothing responded, at least in any fashion that she could recognize.

Then one night the phenomena went to a new level.

Janet awakened at about 3:30 AM, once again, to the faint sounds of violin music. It was always the same piece. "Stop it!" she shouted. "Stop it! Go away!" But the music played on.

Irritated, Janet pushed back the covers and rose to go to the living room. The music halted. As she entered the room, the shadow box containing the antique violin separated from the wall and launched itself through the air at her at tremendous speed. It barely missed her, and crashed to the floor. Janet stared at it. The precious violin was broken in two—but the shadow box and its glass cover were intact. How could that be? The force of the impact was enough to break the violin, which had been mounted and secured inside—but the fragile glass had survived.

Later that day, John's phone rang and he picked up the receiver.

"You don't know me and my name is Janet ____," said a female voice that sounded stressed. "Please don't think I'm crazy. I've got this violin that's haunting my house and I need to get rid of it *now*. Someone told me you take these things. You can have it if you want it, but you'd better get here as soon as you can!"

It took John several minutes to calm Janet down so that she could explain what was going on. He made arrangements to come to her house.

Janet was a munchkin of a woman lost inside an oversized charcoal gray sweater. Her short, curly hair and dark-framed glasses gave her an intellectual look. When John was ushered in, he noticed the chill in the air and had a fleeting glimpse of a shadow that disappeared out of the living room. Janet took him straight to the violin, which was still shattered inside its display box and lying where it had fallen on the floor. "I haven't touched it since it fell," she said. "I was afraid to."

John picked it up and examined it and then looked up at the hook where it had been attached to the wall. How odd that the box was intact, without even a scratch or dent, while the violin was snapped completely in two. He set the box back on the floor.

"It just flew off the wall, I swear," said Janet. "I have never seen anything like it. It was like someone took it and *threw* it." She paused. "But why didn't the box break? Why just the violin?"

John shook his head. "We see things like this all the time," he said. "Something will break in a weird way, or something will get thrown and not break when it should. Do you know anything about where it came from?"

Janet explained how she found the violin in a high-end antique shop. "I was so excited," she said. "As you can see, I like to collect musical instruments. A violin this old and in excellent condition usually sells at auction. It was my understanding that the heirs of this just wanted to get rid of it. I don't know its exact history of ownership, but probably no one famous owned it." She heaved her shoulders. "When I heard the music at night, it was the same piece over and over again—the second movement of the Tchaikovsky Violin Concerto." She looked at John. "It's a mournful piece."

John picked up the shadow box again. As he did so, he had the strong impression that whoever had owned and probably played this violin was still attached to it in some way—and was not happy to see the instrument in this new environment. This attached ghost had the equivalent of a paranormal temper tantrum, creating poltergeist phenomena and breaking other objects, but oddly leaving the collection of musical instruments alone—something a musician might be inclined to do. Perhaps the ghostly former owner hoped Janet would return the violin to the store. When she did not, he broke it in a fit. As for the repeated phantom music, John surmised that it had been a favorite piece of the original owner.

John explained his theory to Janet.

"I never really believed in ghosts," she said, looking down at the floor. "Until now. Will this ghost keep bothering me?"

"Once this is taken out of the house, probably not, but we won't know for certain for a while."

Janet affirmed that she no longer wanted to keep the violin, either in or out of the house. "I can't return it to the store either," she said. "Not in this condition. And who would believe me about what happened?"

John chuckled. "You'd be surprised."

"Well, you can have it for your museum," she said. "But won't it bother you now?"

"I do a clearing on it," he said. "It won't be playing any more music."

The violin was occupied by a residual ghost, created by an intense emotional connection that the original owner had to a beloved instrument. A residual ghost is like a fragment of a person left behind after someone has passed from the earth plane. In clearing the violin, John said prayers for the unknown original owner, assuring him that even though the violin had been broken, it would be well cared for in the museum.

There was a sadness to the case: a soul separated from a cherished possession by the vast gulf between life and death. In all likelihood, the violin had defined a man's life, and leaving it behind was unbearable. Perhaps now, with the binding and the prayers, the fragmented energy would be at peace.

The broken violin still rests, shattered, in its shadow box, deep in the bowels of John's Museum of the Paranormal. It remains silent.

14

Be Careful What You Wish For

Go ahead, rub the lamp a little. Make a wish. It's just a game!

The words kept dancing through Jamie's head, along with the sound of pleasant laughter. Jamie turned the small brown clay lamp over in her hands. It was only a few inches in length and had a rough surface. It had been made to hold oil and a wick in the spout for light. It was old, an antique, and it had come from somewhere in the Middle East—or so Jamie had been told.

Go ahead, urged the voice in her head. *Rub the lamp a little. Make a wish. It's just a game!*

She shook her head as if to clear her mind. Her imagination was running away with her. Well, the lamp did look like a genie lamp, an Aladdin lamp. Wouldn't it be wild if it had a genie inside? Maybe he would be really hot, a bare-chested hunky guy who would do her bidding. Just like the legends!

The moment passed, and Jamie put the little lamp back on her shelf.

The voice in her head did not go away. Jamie found herself thinking about the lamp when there was no reason to think about it. The thoughts intruded on her. The laughter echoed in her head. She had mental visions of an enticing genie man emerging from the lamp in a cloud of smoke and thundering, "Your wish is my command!"

You've watched too many movies, she told herself. *Genies are not real.*

It was a nice fantasy, however, and Jamie did not want to let go of it. She had not had a meaningful relationship in a long time in her thirty-something years, and she was weary of spending her evenings and weekends alone or as a fifth wheel with friends. It couldn't hurt to indulge in a fantasy. She longed for some excitement in her life.

Jamie was about to get more excitement than she could handle.

One Friday night, Jamie came home from work and resigned herself to another night solo in front of the television. She fixed a small supper and then played on the internet for a while, but not for long—God forbid that people "out there" should notice that she had nothing to do on a Friday night. Then she settled in for the long and lonely haul of the evening. She got herself a nosebag of chocolate candies and a diet soda and plunked down on her sofa.

Some stupid monster movie was the only semi-interesting thing on. It barely held her attention.

Bor—ing.

The little lamp on the shelf caught her eye. It seemed to glow in the dim light of the living room.

The mystery voice pierced her thoughts. *Go ahead, rub the lamp a little. Make a wish. It's just a game!* The words were followed by laughter.

Jamie was suddenly seized by an irresistible impulse. *What the hell,* she thought. *Why not?*

She picked up the clay lamp and cradled it in her hands. Yes, rub it and make a wish, that's what the legends said. What should she wish for? The legends said you had three wishes. Somehow they never worked out well in the stories. People wished for the wrong things and were sorry. You had to be careful how you worded the wish. What if she only had one wish and not three? She had to make this one count. She could wish for tons of money. If she had lots of money, that would take care of everything else. Or, she could wish for a dream lover, the perfect husband.

A lightning bolt of inspiration gave her the answer. She should wish for all her wishes to come true.

Jamie rubbed the little lamp and made the wish.

Nothing happened. No smoke poured out of the lamp. No genie materialized. The earth did not shudder in its orbit.

Ah well, Jamie thought. *Ah well.*

That night, Jamie had an odd dream. She was standing in a long line of people that snaked outside of a building. In front of the doorway was a big sign that read, "Free Lunch Today."

The line moved and Jamie was inside the building, which revealed itself as a large cafeteria. She picked up a plate. When she got to the food trays, she started to help herself, but a man behind the counter barked at her to stop.

"What are you doing?" he demanded. He was a swarthy man with a heavy, neatly trimmed black chinstrap beard and moustache. He was quite attractive, and Jamie blushed.

"I'm getting lunch," said Jamie, her cheeks aflame.

"You haven't paid," said the man. He glowered at her.

"But the sign said free—"

He shook his head. "There is no such thing as a free lunch. You can have lunch if you pay. Make me an offer."

Jamie stared blankly at the man.

"I know what you want," he said. His dark eyes glittered.

Suddenly Jamie felt uneasy. *Is this real? Or am I dreaming?* she thought. *If I am dreaming, then I wish I would wake up.*

The dream ended and Jamie awakened.

She was disoriented. The dream had seemed so real, but here she was, in her own bed. What a crazy dream.

Later that morning, she was annoyed at one of her co-workers. She didn't particularly like Sandra, whose fat mouth was always in motion. Sandra had the cubicle next to Jamie's work station, where they both processed paperwork for their insurance company employer. Jamie had never before met anyone who could spend all day talking and say nothing. Jamie's job was drier than dust, and with Miss Motormouth on the other side of the cubicle it was often hard for her to concentrate.

This morning Sandra was blabbering away with another co-worker. The droning went on and on. Jamie put her head down into her hands. *I wish Sandra would stuff it,* she thought.

In less than a minute there were sounds of severe coughing. Jamie stood up. Sandra was doubled over in her chair, coughing like she had something stuck in her throat. She got up and went to the ladies' room, coughing and hacking all the way. When she returned to her cubicle, Sandra looked wrung out. By afternoon, she went home early, not feeling well.

Wow, that was weird, thought Jamie.

That evening, Jamie went through her usual motions of supper and the distraction of television. She chose a romantic movie with plenty of steam and wished that she had something like that in her life.

Sometime in the depths of the night, she roused from sleep—or thought she did—when she felt a solid form slide into bed next to her. It was hard and hairy and felt like a man. Jamie felt herself caressed in a sensual way. Maybe she was still dreaming, but if so, she didn't want it to stop.

Then she got a look in the darkness at the mystery figure. It was the swarthy man from her lunch line dream.

Jamie screamed and flung her arms out. "Who are you?" she shouted. "Get out!"

The man's face loomed closer to hers.

"Go away!" Jamie shouted. "I wish you would go back to wherever you came from!"

The figure vanished, like an evaporating dream, and Jamie was alone. She stayed awake the rest of the night.

From that moment on, there was no more peace in Jamie's house, or in Jamie's world. A heaviness clung to her wherever she went. The air in the house thickened to an invisible pea soup. A sense of foreboding pervaded every room. The temperature suddenly dropped to a freezing cold, and then just as suddenly shoot back up.

At night, Jamie was awakened by clattering noises on the roof, as though an army of sharp-clawed creatures were skittering about. *Raccoons,* she thought. But there were no raccoons, and she knew it.

Sometimes the clattering noises were followed by violent pounding on the walls.

A shadow figure invaded the house. It had a vague human-like outline but had no features or clearly defined limbs. It scudded about from room to room, appearing and disappearing in the blink of an eye. Sometimes at night, Jamie felt prodded in her sleep and awakened to see a blacker-than-black figure standing right up against her bed. She always screamed, and it vanished in a curl of black smoke.

Small objects went missing. Sometimes they turned up in strange locations. A pair of faux pearl earrings disappeared, only to turn up at the top of the trash in Jamie's kitchen bin. Knickknacks went walkabout from room to room. Every time her eyes fell on the little clay lamp, she heard the words in her ear cajoling her to rub the lamp and make a wish. It was now the last thing she wanted to do.

Most disturbing of all were her dreams. She was often pursued by unknown assailants or unseen monsters. There was a repeating dream in which she was ordered to sign a contract, but resisted.

Once Jamie passed near the little clay lamp and it vibrated violently on the shelf, to the point where it seemed in danger of falling off. She clapped a hand over it and felt it pulse like an electronic device. Shocked, she let go of it so fast that she nearly threw it from the shelf. It rattled about and then suddenly went still.

In short order, Jamie was terrified. She spent more and more time out of the house.

There was no relief. A black cloud of misfortune followed her everywhere. She couldn't do anything right. She was absent-minded and clumsy, knocking into things, stubbing her toe, getting bruised a great deal. Several times, she tripped on stairs at work and nearly fell all the way down. She had two near-misses in her car, involving maniac drivers who materialized out of nowhere.

The second near-miss was the breaking point. Jamie stopped at a four-way stop crossroads. There was no one behind her and no one in the oncoming lane. She looked carefully at both cross streets, even though any arriving traffic would have to stop. She had just pushed her tin can compact out into the intersection when a huge black pickup truck roared down on her from the left. The driver did not slow down, let alone stop. Jamie had a split-second vision of the pickup slamming straight into the driver door. She floored the gas pedal and her little car jumped, barely clearing the pickup.

"Crazy bitch!" the driver screamed at her as the pickup passed, and kept on going.

Jamie pulled over to the side of the road and shook for a long time, tears streaming down her face.

Something was dreadfully wrong. The world had turned upside down when she rubbed that lamp.

John was intensely interested when he heard about the little clay lamp. This was an unusual object, and could only mean one thing.

"Should I throw it out?" a nervous Jamie asked over the phone.

"No, don't do that," John said. "You can put it outside. That will probably calm things down until I can get there."

John found the lamp tucked against the side of the house on the patio. It had an innocent air to it, but he knew immediately that for a small object, it presented a big problem.

Jamie looked over his shoulder while he knelt down and picked up the lamp. "I'm afraid to touch it now," she said, "How can you stand to do it?"

"Lots of practice," John said with a laugh. "So where did this come from?"

"My cousin brought it back from a trip to the Holy Land," Jamie said. "My *rich* cousin. They went all over the Middle East—he and his wife are interested in antiquities and ancient history. He said he got it from a dealer, and that it was old. Not ancient, of course, but old."

John noticed that the lamp had black marks of having been used as an oil-burning lamp in the past.

"What's wrong with it?" said Jamie.

"Djinn."

"Gin?" Jamie was puzzled.

"Not *that* gin," John said, laughing again. "Although a glass of it might help. Djinn—D-J-I-N-N. A genie. You've got a genie on your hands."

Jamie was floored and did not know what to say. "But—but I thought genies weren't real," she finally stammered.

"Oh, they're very real," said John, standing up. "You've got one attached to the lamp, and it's not happy."

Jamie recoiled from the lamp as it if held the bubonic plague. "It's not going to get me, is it?"

"It's been trying," said John. "It's looking for a connection with human energy to let it out. Someone attached it to the lamp a long time ago for a purpose. It's had psychic chains on it. When it came over here to this country, and you paid attention to it, the genie spirit woke up."

"They really grant wishes?"

"Those are stories," John said. "It's all about deals with them. They promise to deliver what you want, but they want something, usually human energy, in return."

Jamie sucked in her breath. A lot of things suddenly made sense, and in a most unpleasant way.

"But I told it I wanted it to go away, back to wherever it came from. Why didn't it leave?"

"It went back to the lamp," John said. "You opened a door and then tried to shut it, but the genie has his foot in it."

"How do I get rid of it?"

John recommended that exorcisms be performed on the house and on Jamie. In the meantime, he would bind the genie to the lamp.

"Take it away," Jamie said. "I don't want it near me. I don't ever want to see or think about genies again."

"I have a friend who's an expert on the Djinn," John said. "I'll have her get in touch with you if you want."

Jamie agreed.

The binding of the lamp was difficult due to the strength of the Djinn that was attached to it. John conveyed to the entity that the score was settled—Jamie had generated plenty of emotional energy for it. When the binding was done, John placed the lamp inside a clear acrylic case to prevent anyone from touching or handling it, which would threaten the integrity of the binding.

Two exorcisms were performed on Jamie and her home environment before she felt completely clear of troubling thoughts. Rosemary gave her a short education on the Djinn, which Jamie found both fascinating and frightening. The average person often does not want to know too much about the spirit world, as if knowing about it invites it into one's life. Actually, having knowledge of the spirit world prevents problems from either starting or getting out of hand.

The Djinn may seem like newcomers on the paranormal block, but, as we've noted, they have been around since ancient times. Djinn are like humans—good, bad, indifferent—and the ones hostile to humans are most likely to seek out interaction.

Most Westerners know little, if anything, about Djinn because they never entered the supernatural lore in this part of the world in any significant way. They have operated below the radar. Western culture has treated "genies" in comical ways, as part of slapstick, quirky movies, and goofy cartoon characters. The Djinn are the exact opposite of their caricatures—they are intelligent, crafty, and swift.

Over the centuries, humans around the world have learned how to deal with Djinn, and how to conjure them for magical purposes. Like other spirits, they can be bound to objects, such as lamps, rings, and jewelry. The Djinn do not work for free, however, and if you ask their favor, you must give them something in return. What many Djinn want is to leach the human life force for their own purposes and create problems and pandemonium.

Some of the oldest stories about Djinn are told in the Arabian Nights folk tales, which were translated for Western audiences in the eighteenth and nineteenth centuries. The term "genie" is a French corruption of "Djinn." The story best-known to Westerners is Aladdin and his magical lamp. The genie imprisoned in the lamp bestows favors upon Aladdin in many wishes, far beyond three, when Aladdin liberates him.

Aladdin's story ends happily—he gets the money and the girl—but many other stories on into modern times, and from real life, present a truer picture of deals usually gone bad: requests (wishes) twisted into disasters, and generations of families cursed by pestering entities who are determined to collect on their deal.

Both of us are well familiar with Djinn and have encountered them many times in various kinds of cases that we have taken on. We have seen serious consequences of health and fortune when people wind up on the wrong side of Djinn. John learned about them from his uncle, Ed Warren. Ed knew the difference between demons and genies, as he called the Djinn. Rosemary realized the immense involvement of the Djinn in paranormal phenomena when she started studying them in 2004, documenting their web of activities in persistent negative hauntings, possessions, bedroom invasions, cryptids (mysterious creatures), and alien abductions.

The Djinn are one of many kinds of entities that can attach to objects. Jamie was fortunate that her situation did not get completely out of hand. She was an aimless wisher, spinning fantasies, unaware that invisible ears were listening. Like many people, she also was unaware of how often the words "I wish" crept into her thoughts and words.

Dealing with Djinn—or any spirit—is no game. The next time you start to say, "I wish..." pause and think it through. Be careful what you wish for.

15

The Scornful Military Jacket

At age twenty-one, Riley was a willowy five-foot-seven with short dark hair and amber-specked brown eyes. From an early age, she had always preferred boyish clothes, and loved the tailored look. The day she found the old gray military jacket at an estate sale marked a big score.

"How old is this?" Riley asked the person running the sale. She held up the jacket.

The man shrugged. "I don't know. Really old. It's the real thing, you know."

Riley was fascinated by the jacket. It was in excellent condition. It was a cutaway in the front and had swallow tails in the back. The brass ball buttons on the front, neck, tails, and sleeves had lots of shine. The black braid was in fine shape. The sleeves were also decorated with three stripes of gold brocade. The collar was faded a bit, and it looked there had once been a name on the inside, but the letters were illegible.

Cool! A real military jacket, not a costume or a fashion knock-off. Riley slipped it on and it fit like a glove. What a great look. Done! She purchased it and walked away wearing it. She was so excited that she did not notice that she felt chilly with the jacket on, even though the day was warm.

The military jacket immediately became her go-to coat. She wore it nearly every day. Even her mother, Connie, commented on it.

"Do you live in that jacket now?" Connie asked one morning when Riley showed up in the kitchen for a quick breakfast. Riley lived at home with her parents while she was finishing college.

"It's awesome," Riley said, pouring herself a glass of orange juice. "Everybody I know wants one like it."

"The young man who once wore it might have died for his country, and he might not appreciate you turning into a fashion piece," Connie said.

"Then why was it for sale, Mom? Did you ever think about that? You can't tell someone how they can use something after they buy it. If anyone wanted the jacket on display, they should have given it to a museum." Riley drained the glass and headed for the door.

"You have to eat something!" Connie called after her.

"Gotta stay thin, Mom," came the answer, and Riley was gone.

A change in the air hit the house that evening. Riley came home late, having gone out with friends for an evening of food and drink.

As usual, her parents were already in bed and probably asleep. She turned off the lights in the living room and headed to her room at the end of the hall. She had that part of the house to herself; the master bedroom where her parents slept was on the other side.

Riley slipped off her prized jacket and hung it on a sturdy wooden hanger on the coat rack in the corner of her room opposite the foot of her bed. She liked to see it instead of putting it away in her closet.

As she turned away from the coat rack, she thought she saw a dark silhouetted figure of a man standing in her room. The figure was gone almost as soon as she saw it. She blinked a few times and decided it must have been the way the hall light was slanting into the room. Her eyes had played tricks on her.

That night, Riley had an unusual dream. It was intense and vivid. She was crouched down in a deep trench. It was dark, but she could make out the outlines of trees in the distance, like the edge of a forest. Around her were sounds of machine gun fire and the whistling sounds of mortars flying through the air, followed by explosions that deafened her and shook the ground. Somewhere in the stench and smoke-filled air were men shouting and screaming in agony. She hugged the edge of the trench and peered over the edge through heavy goggles. She was breathing from a can attached to a mask on her face. She was filled with dread that something terrible was about to happen.

Riley came awake with her heart pounding. She was relieved to find herself in her own bedroom, safe in her cozy bed. What a strange dream! Like she got plunged into some battle scene from a world war.

She settled back down under the covers, punched up her pillows and rolled over. Just as she did so, a dark movement caught the corner of her eye. She looked, wide-eyed, breath caught in her throat, but saw nothing.

In the morning, Riley looked a bit rumpled, even under her military jacket. She had added some fashion pins to the front of it.

"Stay out too late?" asked Connie.

Riley shrugged. "Couldn't sleep very well."

"Something on your mind?"

Riley shrugged again and poured a glass of orange juice.

Connie changed the subject. "You're going to wear that jacket out already," she said.

"So what? I might die tomorrow so I might as well enjoy it today." As soon as the words were out, Riley thought it was an odd thing to say.

Her mother thought it was odd, too, but said nothing.

That night, the shadow figure returned. So did the disturbing dream. This time, the dread that came over Riley was a certainty that she was going to die. She was wrung out and exhausted upon awakening.

Riley dressed, grabbed her military jacket, and headed out her bedroom door. Just as she did, a dark figure zipped down the hallway. When she looked directly up and down the hall, there was nothing to be seen.

Fortunately, she did not have to talk over her "breakfast" of gulped orange juice. Her father always got up and left for work early, before Riley got up. Today her mother was not in the kitchen. Riley hurried to get out of the house. She didn't feel like talking, and didn't want a lecture about getting enough sleep, or wearing out the jacket.

That night, Riley prayed she would not have the same dream again. She saw the shadow figure several times, in the hall and in her bedroom. It always vanished as soon as she caught sight of it.

She had the same dream: the deep trench, the gunfire and explosions, heavy smoke, a horrible, choking stench in the air, and men screaming. Again, she was filled with dread that she was going to die. This time, a deafening explosion hit close by and rained dirt and debris on her. When she looked down at her hands, they were covered in blood. She tried to scream, but no sound came out.

She awoke with the stifled scream still in her throat.

Riley sat up in bed and put her palm on her forehead. It was hot and covered with a film of perspiration. *What's going on?* She wondered. *This sucks.* Just then, the dark form flitted out of her room and zipped down the hall.

Riley could not hide the stress that was written all over her young face when she emerged from her room in the morning.

Her mother was in the kitchen drinking coffee.

"Riley, I want to talk to you."

Bad sign. Riley's stomach tightened. Was she out too much? Spending too much?

The topic of Connie's concern was completely unexpected. "Something strange is going on in this house and I want to know if you have noticed it, too."

"Like what?"

"Sit down." Her mother used her coffee mug to wave her to a chair at the kitchen table.

"I can't, I'll be late."

"You can be late." Connie arched an eyebrow. "It won't be the first time."

Riley slid into a chair and hunched into it.

"I've been seeing odd… shadows," said Connie. "I don't know what else to call them. At first I think a man has come into the house, although all I see is a black silhouette. As soon as I see it, it disappears."

"Yeah, I've seen it, too," admitted Riley, keeping her eyes down on the tabletop. "In my room and in the hall."

Connie looked alarmed, as though the confirmation was not what she wanted to hear. "Has anything else been going on?"

Riley told her about the dreams. "What if they mean I'm going to die?" she said, glancing at Connie. She looked small and afraid, hunched into the chair.

"You're not going to die," Connie said. "Your dream sounds like World War I. Have you seen any World War I movies lately?

Riley shook her head.

"It's the jacket."

"What?" Riley wished her mother would not talk in riddles.

"None of this happened before you brought that jacket into the house." Connie pointed to it lying on the table. "There's something bad about that jacket. I think it's haunted, and you've picked up the memories of the man who wore it."

"No way!" said Riley, grabbing at her jacket and pulling it closer to her.

"I saw a TV show on that once," said Connie. "About how things like clothes and jewelry and personal possessions can be haunted by their former owners. I even saw a show about how some organ transplant people take on the personalities of the person who donated the organ."

"Oh, that's just totally wrong."

"I want that jacket out of the house, Riley," Connie said. "Take it back or give it away."

"No," Riley protested. "First of all, it cost a lot of money and I'll never find another one like it, and I can't take it back, anyway, because it came from a yard sale. I'm not getting rid of it!"

"Put that thing out in the garage. We'll see what happens then." At Riley's defiant look, Connie added, "As long as you live in our house you will do as I say."

Reluctantly, Riley took the jacket out to the garage. She fetched a plastic garment bag from her room and placed it inside, zipping it up. Then she folded it neatly and put it on one the storage racks lining one side of the garage.

"Hey, Captain Riley, where's your uniform," her friends joked when she showed up without it.

Riley put on a face. "Got boring," she said. "I'm giving it a rest."

That night, there were no dark figures in the hall or her bedroom. Riley stayed up later than usual, playing on the computer, afraid to go to sleep. At last fatigue got the better of her, and she slipped beneath the covers.

She did not have "the dream."

As suddenly as the phenomena started, the phenomena stopped. No dark figures haunted the house. Riley's dreams went back to normal.

Connie noticed the change, too, but would not allow the jacket back in the house. "And you're not wearing it, either, even from the garage," Connie said to Riley.

"It can't stay out there forever, Mom," Riley said.

"Let it be for a while. Let's see."

And so the military jacket sat folded in the garage for several weeks. The house—and Riley—remained clear.

Connie still would not allow the jacket back in the house. Riley refused to dispose of it, and so the jacket remained in limbo...

...Until Riley decided to secrete it back into the house. One night after her parents had gone to bed, Riley quietly took a jacket out of her closet, tiptoed to the garage, and switched it with the military jacket. The garment bag was opaque, so as long as she kept the jacket out of sight, no one would be the wiser for the switch.

She put the military jacket on a hanger in the back of her closet. There were all sorts of ways that she could get it out of the house unnoticed— under a coat or wrap, in her gym bag, her back pack, even her oversized tote bag that she often used for a purse.

As soon as Riley brought the jacket back into the house, a palpable shift occurred to the atmosphere: there was a feeling of foreboding.

Riley noticed, but went into denial. There was nothing wrong with the jacket. Whatever had been affecting the house was gone now.

As she drifted off to sleep, a rustling noise roused her and she opened her eyes in time to see a shadow figure dart out of her bedroom and go down the hall. She caught her breath and then decided, *Just my imagination,* and rolled over and went to sleep. And dreamed.

It was the same deep trench. The earth was cold and muddy where water had seeped in. Chaos. Screaming. Gunfire and explosions. Riley was slumped against the side of the trench. She felt blood rushing from her body, and knew she was going to die.

Once again, she awakened with a scream stuck in her throat.

In the morning, a knock sounded on her bedroom door. It was her mother.

"I saw that shadow thing this morning," Connie said, standing in the partially open doorway. "Did you bring that coat back into the house?"

"No," Riley lied.

Connie opened the door wider and held up the garment bag that Riley had used to store the jacket in the garage. "Then would you like to explain why there's another jacket in this bag?"

Riley looked sullen and slid out of bed. She went to her closet and fished out the military jacket. "I didn't think it would do any harm," she said. "I thought all that stuff was over."

Connie took the jacket from her. "We're going to get to the bottom of this."

A few days later, Connie handed the jacket to John as they sat at her kitchen table and drank coffee. Riley hovered in the background, not wanting to be present. The two women had just finished telling the details to John about the activity in the house, and Riley's dreams.

"This is a West Point jacket," John said. "You got a good one. Old." He looked at the front, back and insides. "Can't make out the name, which is too bad. We could track down the history of the owner if we had it."

"Was it ever worn in battle?" Connie asked. "Is that why Riley had that dream every night?"

"This is a cadet's dress jacket," John said. "It would not have been worn into combat. But that doesn't mean that whoever owned it did not see fighting. He probably did, and he may have even died in battle. He's left an emotional attachment behind, and part of him is still linked to this jacket, which represented an important accomplishment in his life."

John asked Riley if she could remember any more details about her dream.

She thought a moment. "I kept hearing a strange word in my head," she said. "It sounded like... eepers. Like jeepers creepers only eepers."

"That sounds like World War I, all right," John said. "There was a place in Belgium by that name where many battles took place and lots of lives were lost, including Americans. They used chlorine gas, which is a horrible way to die. Maybe our West Point soldier died there."

The idea gave Riley the shivers.

"This soldier wants to be at rest," John said.

Riley gave the jacket to John. "I can't wear it any more, she said.

Back home, John said a series of prayers for the unknown soldier who originally owned the jacket. The soldier was not earthbound, but an emotional piece of him was left behind with the jacket. Without a name, there was no way to know for certain what happened to him, or the exact age of the jacket. West Point Military Academy jackets have not changed in design since the 1800s, with the exception of the introduction of a wool and polyester blend fabric to replace all-wool. Riley's jacket appeared to be all wool and had age on it, and could easily have dated to the early twentieth century. The cadet dress jackets would have been worn on various occasions at the academy in New York State.

When no name is known, John says general prayers that acknowledge the person has passed on, that their item has been properly taken care of, and they can cross into the light. Even fragments of a soul can be reunited with the dead.

Our theory: the original owner was a young man who was passionate about a military career. Acceptance into West Point was the ultimate honor, and the dress jacket was a symbol of that glory. The young man graduated and entered the armed forces, and was sent into active duty in Europe when the United States entered World War I in 1917. Americans fought in many locations, including the famous Ypres, Belgium area, where a series of five battles were fought between 1914 and 1918, at a cost of nearly one million lives in soldiers alone. Chlorine gas killed many of them. (Note: Ypres is pronounced ee'-pres, but the British and Americans pronounced it ee'-pers, the word that Riley heard in her dream.)

The young man's military career and life were tragically cut short. Part of him could not let go of the one thing that linked him to the most important part of his life. When Riley acquired the jacket and turned it into a fashion statement, there was enough energy attached to the jacket to erupt in protest.

That energy is now laid to rest.

16

Don't Call Him Pig Face

Kimberley awakened from the nightmare drenched in sweat. It was happening again.

The street lamps from outside the apartment penetrated the window blinds, creating a dim light in the bedroom. Kim's eyes were immediately drawn to a wall shelf, held by brackets, on one side of the room. There sat Pig Face, a large statue of a man with a strange, pig-like face. The eyes were bright and sharp, and looked straight at her with an eerie intelligence. A shiver went through her.

Kim looked at the digital clock on the night stand. It read 3:15 AM. Beside her, Ned, her boyfriend, slept peacefully, snoring lightly and oblivious to her distress.

Kim rolled onto one side to turn her back on Pig Face. In her mind, she heard the words, *Don't turn your back on me!* as though Pig Face could get into her head.

Don't be stupid, she thought to herself. *You're imagining things. It must be the nightmare.*

Sleep, however, would not come. Kim tossed and turned and could not get over the feeling that Pig Face was watching her. At last she got up and fled the bedroom without looking at the figure.

"Bad night again, hunh," Ned said as he poured himself a mug of coffee in their tiny galley kitchen. It was more a comment than a question.

Kim sat scrunched on the sofa in the small living room on the other side of the kitchen counter. Her mass of straight, ebony hair was in disarray. Her feet were on the sofa and her knees were pulled up to her chin, and her arms were wrapped around her folded legs. She grunted an affirmative answer.

"You've been having the same nightmare every night for a couple of weeks now," Ned said in a grim tone.

Kim nodded. It was always the same. The nightmare was a hellish drama and Kim was dropped into the middle of it. An unseen but horrible monster was pursuing her, and she knew that something quite terrifying would happen to her if it captured her. She stumbled around in a dark and alien landscape, with the monster drawing closer and closer. A paralysis always set in, and Kim found herself moving slower and slower, as though she were struggling through invisible molasses. She tried to scream, but sound stuck in her throat. She awakened just as the monster was about to get her.

The first thing she always saw upon awakening was Pig Face, his eyes riveted upon her as if to say, *You finally got my message.*

The very thought of the nightmare made Kim shiver. "He's getting into my head," she said. She didn't specify the "he" but Ned knew exactly what she meant. "I can hear him talking in my mind." She paused and fingered her black pajamas decorated with happy little pink pigs, an odd irony. "He even knows what I do. Last night, when I rolled over, I heard him tell me not to turn my back on him."

Ned made an exasperated noise, set down his coffee mug and disappeared into the bedroom. He returned holding Pig Face and waved it in front of her.

"This! This is the problem! I told you I didn't like it and didn't want it, but you insisted on having it. There's something *wrong* with it, Kim. Get rid of it!"

Kim kept her head down but cast her eyes mournfully up at Ned.

"Get rid of this damn Pig Face!" Ned shouted.

"Don't call him Pig Face," Kim protested in a small voice. "He doesn't like it."

"He doesn't like it? I'll call him whatever I damn well want!" Ned stepped on the pedal of the metal waste bin by the counter and hovered the statue over it.

"Don't!" said Kim.

Ned shot her an icy look and slammed the statue down on the counter. "I'm late for work," he snapped. "We'll talk about this later." Within minutes he was gone.

The problem that now gripped the little apartment occupied by Kim and Ned had started several weeks earlier. On a road trip out of town, the couple passed by an antique emporium and decided to stop in. Both of them loved odd things that drew the attention of others. Both of them were fascinated by the supernatural, and participated in ghost hunts and rituals to welcome the changes of season. They had tried different forms of spirit communication with their friends. It all seemed harmless and good fun. People always commented that Kim was a magnet for spirits and could draw them in. She liked that, but was never motivated to learn more about the spirit world, how to deal with it—or how to keep it out. She would have been wise to learn.

Kim's Native American heritage played a prominent role in the couple's interests, too. Many Native American items were part of the couple's eclectic occult interests. Their little one-bedroom apartment housed numerous trophies that they discovered here and there.

At the antique emporium, Kim's attention was drawn to a statue of a man dressed in a rumpled red suit. It was about a foot high. The face looked almost animal in nature, with a broad, flat and upturned nose. It was hard to discern whether it was a man with a weird face, or some sort of human-like but supernatural entity.

When she picked it up, a surge went through her. She felt compelled to buy it.

Ned was not so taken with the statue. He found it grotesque and unappealing. "It's a guy with a pig face," he said disdainfully. "Straight out of the devil's hopyard. It looks like a reject from an amateur art class."

Kim prevailed, and the pig-faced man went home with them. For reasons even Kim could not explain, she placed the figure in their bedroom instead of in the living room with the bulk of their collection. Ned grumbled about it but let it be.

Soon after the figure was installed at home, both Ned and Kim noticed a change in the "vibe" of the place. The very air felt oppressive and heavy. At first, neither of them mentioned the change to the other. Then comments were made.

"It's probably that Pig Face," Ned said in an offhand manner. He had called the figure "Pig Face" from the beginning, which rankled Kim. He said it so often that in her mind she began referring to it as Pig Face as well. It seemed appropriate, even if it was disrespectful, she thought. The man really did have a pig-like face.

Ned disliked the statue, but was not as affected by it as Kim. To her, Pig Face was animated in a bizarre way. It watched her. It conveyed impressions to her. She found herself talking to it as though it were a real person.

The scary thing was, Pig Face talked back.

Kim, look at me, it would say. *Look at me.*

Then the nightmares started. Along with the nightmares came a feeling that a heavy force was pressing on Kim physically. She felt it when she awakened from the nightmares, and also at other times, too. If her eyes fell on Pig Face, she immediately felt the pressure.

The pressure grew in strength. It seemed that something was trying to get inside her.

Kim descended into a prison of terror. She felt powerless to do anything in her own defense. Whatever hold Pig Face had on her could not be broken.

After Ned arrived home from work that night, the couple got into an intense argument over Pig Face. For Ned, both the problem and the solution were simple: weird and unpleasant things started when Pig Face came into the home. Get rid of Pig Face, end of problem.

Kim would not let it go.

"This is creeping me out, Kim," Ned said. "I don't like what's going on, and I don't like what has happened to you. You're not even the same person anymore. It's like you're—you're *possessed.*"

"I am *not* possessed!"

"Then let's get rid of it."

"No!"

"There's nothing stopping me from taking a hammer to it," Ned said defiantly.

"You wouldn't!"

"I'm about to—"

"I'll never talk to you again!"

Ned leveled a steely gaze at her. "If you won't listen to me, maybe you'll listen to someone else."

"What, my mother?" Kim said. "You're not going to get *her* involved." Kim's mother possessed a great deal of knowledge about the spirit world, but Kim did not want her meddling in her affairs.

"Not your mother," Ned replied. "The *godfather*."

Ned was referring to John, the "Godfather of the Paranormal."

John arrived at the apartment after having been briefed by Ned on the phone. Ned's young face was creased with worry. Kim looked much older than her twenty-something years, which John saw as the effects of supernatural oppression. Her energy field was hollow and depleted. She had a sullen look and her eyes were dull.

"This is it, what I was telling you about," said Ned, thrusting the figure at John. "Pig Face."

John noticed that Kim recoiled at the name. Not a good sign.

He examined the figure. It was handmade out of ceramic and was crudely hand painted. There was most definitely a spirit attached to it. This one was no low-level trickster, but a powerful entity. John wondered if the figure had been made by someone for the express purpose of housing a familiar.

Ned and Kim could shed no light on the object's past history. The antiques emporium was a collection of stalls that were rented out, and the clerks behind the checkout desk knew nothing.

John explained to the couple how objects can sometimes attract spirits which attach to them and then act out in a new environment, especially if there are psychically sensitive people in residence. Kim certainly fit that profile. Given that the object was handmade and unusual in appearance, someone involved in the occult may have made it especially to house a spirit that would serve as a regular companion and servant. Perhaps this figure had never been properly deactivated, or, something had happened to the owner, and the statue had been passed along in sale of the estate. Along came Kim, who felt attracted to the object, and had the right psychic sensitivity for the spirit to become energized and active.

Hearing this, Ned had an I-told-you-so expression. Kim looked as though she did not want to acknowledge any of it, especially her role in the problem.

"This statue should be deactivated," John said. "At the very least, you should get it out of the apartment."

Kim had been silent so far, but now she spoke up. "I don't want to get rid of it," she said. "How would you deactivate it so I can keep it?"

John explained the process, adding. "I have to warn you, sometimes activity will increase after that. Things might get worse before they get better, especially if the object is not taken away."

He proceeded to sprinkle Pig Face with holy water and sea salt, and then said prayers over the statue. "Let me know what happens," he said.

After John departed, an eerie calm settled over the apartment. It was like a calm before a storm.

That night, Kim had the repeating nightmare. This time, she awakened feeling pinned to the bed by a heavy but invisible weight on top of her. It was suffocating her. She struggled violently against it and succeeded in throwing it off of her. She fell back onto the bed gasping for air.

The tumult awakened Ned. In the midst of the chaos, the sound of something crashing to the floor and breaking into smithereens sounded from the living room. Ned and Kim ran out to investigate, but could find nothing amiss. Everything was in place and accounted for.

In a few days, John received a phone call, this time from Kim instead of Ned. In a halting voice, she described how the activity in the apartment was worse than ever.

"This horrible weight is now hitting me whenever I try to go to sleep at night," Kim said.

"You've got to get that statue out of there," John urged.

There were a few moments of silence on the other end. "Okay," Kim said. "I'll put it in the basement."

That was not an ideal solution, either, but John could not convince her otherwise.

The apartment building had a basement storage area, and all apartments were assigned a locker. Pig Face was relocated to the one assigned to Ned and Kim.

For a short time, the apartment felt clear, as though the air had been cleaned. The peace ended that very night.

Kim awakened once again from the same nightmare. This time, she heard a voice in her head. *Help me... help me... don't leave me here...* She knew it was Pig Face, calling to her from the depths of the basement.

The voice continued into the day. It followed her to work and wherever she went. *Come and get me... don't leave me... help me...* it wailed piteously.

The voice would not stop. It went on for days and nights. There was nothing Kim could do to keep it out of her head. It was driving her insane.

The voice started telling her to get rid of Ned. *He doesn't like me... He wants to hurt me... I want you all to myself,* Pig Face said.

Finally Kim relented. Of course she would never get rid of Ned, but she had to stop the pestering voice. She went down to the basement. When she opened the locker, there was Pig Face, glaring at her in an accusatory way. She picked him up and brought him back to the apartment, reinstalling him in his former place on the bedroom shelf.

Ned was furious, but to no avail.

Restoring Pig Face did not bring relief. Instead, the spirit attached to the statue seemed bent on revenge for being banished. Kim was physically attacked, and huge bruises appeared all over her arms and legs.

Now thoroughly terrified by a situation completely out of control, Kim contacted John again. This time, she begged him to take Pig Face away. John came quickly and removed it.

He subjected Pig Face to a thorough cleansing and binding outside of his home, and when the object was clear, he placed it inside the Museum of the Paranormal. Pig Face would bother no one again.

Meanwhile, Kim suffered a near breakdown as a result of the paranormal activity and assaults. She did something else she had resisted— she contacted her mother.

Her mother, a Native American, arranged for a shaman within the tribal community to perform an exorcism and blessing upon the apartment and Kim.

Kim also had more consultations with John. Weeks later, she finally felt free and clear of the emotional residual of Pig Face.

Kim did not escape casualties, however. Ned announced that he was done with their relationship. The toll on him had been heavy, too. He felt deeply betrayed by Kim's willingness to expose both of them to risk.

"You need to get yourself straightened out," he told Kim. He packed his belongings and left.

Perhaps Pig Face won after all. The spirit was bound and neutralized, but spirits can wait a very long time, longer than human lifetimes, if necessary. There will always be another target, somewhere... sometime.

Pig Face demonstrates how a paranormal situation can rapidly escalate beyond control. It also demonstrates the vulnerability some people have concerning the spirit world. Kim, who had more than average psychic sensitivity, was more affected than Ned.

We all have barriers in place in the form of our aura of vitality, and the spiritual shielding that comes from having a spiritual foundation and practice. It is foolish to dabble around in the spirit world without taking the time to know what you are dealing with and how to protect yourself properly from side effects. Kim was told repeatedly by friends that she was a spirit magnet, yet she never took it seriously enough to educate and train herself. She also neglected the wonderful resource in her mother's knowledge, and turned to her barely in time.

Had the situation progressed, Kim might have found herself under a full-scale possession. The process of exorcism and recovery becomes much more complicated at that point, often requiring multiple treatments over a prolonged period of time. Scars and after-effects can linger for years.

Kim was fortunate. She got her life back, even though she lost a relationship in the process.

Once a situation is resolved, we rarely hear from people again. In Kim's case, we hope she was motivated to regain control of the spiritual and psychic sides of her life.

17

Jewelry Cursed By A Jilted Witch

Nathan got in his car and headed out to the condo of his fiancée, Kate. Tonight was going to be the toughest night of his life, for he was going to break the engagement. He wasn't pleased about it, or with himself, but he had no alternative. He could not marry a witch.

Actually, he was justified, he told himself as he drove along. Kate had not been honest with him, hadn't revealed that about herself until recently. It certainly explained a lot of things, though. Over the course of their relationship, Kate's behavior changed, and to Nathan, she became increasing unstable and unpredictable. She said she was following the will of the gods, but Nathan could not fathom why any god would turn a woman into a female Jekyll and Hyde.

Nor did he understand what she practiced. She claimed it wasn't Wicca, but some secret tradition passed down through her family line. To Nathan, the distinction was meaningless.

Kate told Nathan that her family members, as well as herself, possessed powers that most people did not have. She related stories about how people were frightened of her family. No one dared cross them, she said. She made jokes about how he better watch his step.

Nathan tried to act nonchalant about the witchcraft revelation, but he didn't succeed. The more time went on, the more he did not like what was happening in the relationship. He was tired of the drama, done with it, and honestly, bottom line, he didn't want anything to do with someone who dabbled in sorcery. He tried to let the relationship taper off, but she possessed some sort of tractor beam that always pulled him back in. Before he knew it, he had agreed to marriage.

Marriage was not going to happen. Tonight he was ending it, once and for all.

Kate had a forest of candles going inside the dimly lit condo. *What was she planning?* Nathan wondered as he stepped through the door. He gave her a half-hearted hug and kiss.

"I thought we would—" Kate began.

"Kate, we have to talk."

Kate did not take Nathan's news well. She cried, she yelled. Nathan was distressed and extremely uncomfortable. She asked him over and over why he was backing out. He gave her different reasons: he wasn't ready to be married; he was thinking of taking a job in another state. Finally he said, "We have different outlooks on life, and I don't think they are ever going to mesh."

Kate's lipped thinned. "I see." She removed her pink sapphire engagement ring and threw it at Nathan.

He picked the ring up off the floor and handed it back to her. "I want you to keep it," he said. "Wear it, sell it, do whatever you want with it."

She refused to take it and so he set it down on the sofa. He fumbled around in his jacket pocket and withdrew a small wooden box. It was inlaid with geometric patterns in black and white. It had been a gift from Kate, and she had told him the inlay was done in bone. When he asked what kind of bone, she just laughed and said he didn't want to know.

He held it toward her. "I think it would be right for you to have these, too." Inside were several pieces of jewelry that Kate had given him: a gold ring set with a large garnet; a silver bracelet of heavy links; and cufflinks made of mixed yellow and white gold, set with blue star sapphires.

Kate took the box and cupped it in her hands. She closed her eyes and seemed to withdraw into deep thought. Then she opened her eyes and opened the box, looked inside, and closed the lid. She gave the box back to Nathan. "No, these are meant to stay with you," she said.

Something in her tone and the way she held the box unnerved Nathan. He decided it would be easier for him to exit if he took the jewelry back.

That would prove to be a mistake.

Nathan promised to stay in touch and affirmed that they would always be friends, even though he knew it was a transparent lie. Lovers never break up and remain friends. They go their separate ways.

Days, weeks, and then months went by, and Kate faded from Nathan's thoughts. They never talked or called each other. He had no idea where she was or what she was doing. He would always feel badly about how the relationship ended, but, on the other hand, he was relieved he had gotten out of it. Married to a witch—no way!

Eventually Nathan met and fell in love with another woman. They made plans to marry, and his energy was consumed with building a new life. He told Nicki about Kate, but omitted her witchy lifestyle. No need to raise unnecessary concerns.

Nicki was in her mid-twenties, almost a decade younger than Nathan, and she wanted a showy, fairy book wedding with all the trimmings. Her family had the means to stage one. Nathan was drawn into months of elaborate planning. He had no idea weddings could be so complicated. Before he knew it, the guest list was more than 100 persons and still growing. The wedding was going to be held in the best luxury hotel in town, and the honeymoon promised to be a dream come true. Nathan's future father-in-law told him he wanted to make sure his little girl was going to be happy.

Nathan had no doubt about that—they were madly in love. Nicki eclipsed Kate in all respects.

Everything went perfectly, without a hitch—until the wedding night.

When Nathan and Nicki were finally able to make their escape from the celebration, they sank into the huge bridal bed at the hotel, eager for a night of passionate lovemaking. They had been intimate during their relationship, but both had savored the moment of making their union physically official.

They were not far into it when it became obvious that Nathan was not going to be able to perform. He was embarrassed and humiliated. Of all times, on his wedding night!

Nicki could not hide her disappointment, but she assured him it was no big deal. They could have sex later, in the middle of the night, or in the morning.

"Too much champagne," Nathan mumbled, still upset.

They fell into a restless sleep.

In the middle of the night, Nathan awakened to Nicki pushing him.

"Stop it!" she said.

"Hunh? Stop what? Whatsamatter?"

"Stop hurting me!"

"What?" Nathan was now awake. "I'm not doing anything. I was sleeping."

"You were pinching me and slapping me," Nicki insisted.

"No I wasn't."

"Well, somebody was, and there's nobody here but you."

Nathan switched on the bedside light and looked at Nicki. Her hair was disheveled. She held out an arm. "Look." There were red welts on it.

Nathan did not know what to say. "You must have bumped the table or something in your sleep or slept on it wrong," he said. "I was sound asleep. I swear."

"I didn't hit the table," Nicki said. "I woke up being pinched and hit. This isn't funny, Nathan."

Nathan ran his fingers through his hair. "Nicki, you know I would never hurt you, not in any way. I don't understand."

"I don't either. If this is a joke, I want it to stop."

"Hey, let's cool it," Nathan said, reaching out for her. "It must have been a bad dream."

They cuddled but Nathan still could not perform, to his chagrin. Soon they drifted off to sleep again.

Next it was Nathan's turn to come awake to the sensation of being pinched and pummeled. He yelled and jumped out of bed, causing Nicki to wake up with a shriek.

"I thought I was being attacked," he said. "Like someone had broken into the room."

"I don't know what's going on," said Nicki, "but I don't like it. Are you sure one of your friends isn't hiding in here, trying to play a bad joke on us?"

"Don't be ridiculous."

They tossed and turned the rest of the night. In the morning, a strained feeling lay between them, and there was no official consummation of the marriage then, either. Nicki looked even more disappointed, but said little.

The honeymoon was a mix of hot and cold. It should have been a dream trip for lovers, but it became increasingly stressful. During the day, everything was superficially fine. Every time they attempted to make love, however, something happened. Nathan had more performance difficulties, a problem that had never plagued him in the past. Nicki had problems, too—she fell and sprained her ankle. It swelled to an enormous size and was intensely painful. The couple had to curtail their sightseeing.

Whenever they slept at night, they were both attacked with pinching and hitting by some invisible force. Nathan was at a loss to explain it, and was unable to do anything to protect himself and his bride.

By the end of the honeymoon, Nicki was distant. Nathan feared she was regretting getting married.

"Look," he told her, "maybe we're both stressed out from the wedding and getting adjusted to being married. Maybe we're having realistic nightmares. Let's get home and relax. Everything will be fine."

Unfortunately, nothing changed when they got home. Instead, their situation got worse.

Before the wedding, Nathan and Nicki had purchased a spacious condo in a trendy district in the city. It offered great views and was in the heart of an area filled with popular restaurants, night clubs, and shops. Nathan was convinced that once they moved in and settled into their new lifestyle, normalcy would reinstate itself. He was wrong.

From their first night, the attacks continued. Nicki was clearly out of sorts. She withdrew from Nathan and was edgy and irritable. Nathan wasn't doing much better.

One morning Nicki arose and walked into the master bathroom, and screamed. Nathan rushed in, finding Nicki huddled against one wall, shielding her eyes. Without looking up, she pointed to the mirror.

The mirror had foul words scrawled on it in capital letters in a jagged, uneven hand, as though someone had taken a magic marker pen and defaced the glass. In the lower left-hand corner, the word "KILL" was written backwards.

"Why do you keep tormenting me?" Nicki said, crying. "Why did you ever marry me?"

"I'm not doing this," Nathan said, but his words were drowned out by Nicki's sobbing.

Nicki confided to her mother what was going on, and soon Nathan had more trouble, a pair of irate in-laws, who demanded that he seek counseling. Nicki's mother urged her to come home until Nathan straightened out, but Nathan persuaded Nicki to stay. He was desperate for a solution.

Then he found John.

"I really need help, man," he told John over the phone. "I just got married and I'm about to lose my wife, as well as my sanity. I don't know what's happening."

Nathan and Nicki lived halfway across the country, so John did the consulting by phone. He interviewed Nathan for details. Neither Nathan nor Nicki had the pattern of life-long paranormal experiencers, yet the activity had followed them from one location to another. They had no medical issues and were not involved in the occult.

"Did you buy anything unusual, or acquire anything secondhand right before the attacks started?" John asked.

"We bought a lot of things for the condo," Nathan said. "I can't think of anything unusual. We have picked up a few things second hand, but all of those were bought since we got home from the honeymoon."

"Is there any reason why someone would be mad at you?" John asked.

Nathan thought for a moment. "No...oh, wait." He paused. "Before I met Nicki, I was engaged to someone else. Maybe..."

"What happened there?" John said.

"I broke it off," Nathan answered. "I haven't had any contact with her since then, so I don't see how... I mean, if she was mad at me, I'd have heard from her—wouldn't I?"

"Why did you break it off?"

"You're going to think this is crazy, but... she said she was a witch, and I... well, she was weird, too weird for me."

"A witch?" This was a missing crucial piece of the puzzle. "What kind of a witch?"

Nathan did not give a direct answer. "I never really believed her..."

"That's okay, just tell me what she said about herself, or what she did," said John.

Nathan told John everything he knew about Kate. He felt silly, as though talking about it gave her credence.

"All right," John said, when Nathan was finished. "Now step me through what happened when you broke up with her."

Nathan described the last evening with Kate. "She didn't want to keep the ring, but I wouldn't take it," he said. "I thought that was right. She could sell it if nothing else. I tried to give her back the jewelry she had given me, but she wouldn't take it, so I kept it."

Another missing crucial piece of the puzzle fell into place. "Tell me about the jewelry," John said.

Nathan described the bracelet, ring, and cufflinks. "They were nice," he said. "She had good taste. I'm not much on jewelry, but I wore them every now and then to make her happy. I had them in a little wood box—that was also a present from her—but she wouldn't take them, said they were meant to stay with me."

"Did she handle any of the pieces?"

Nathan was silent a moment. "She held the box for a minute or two, like she was trying to decide what to do. Then she handed it back to me." He hastened to add, "I put everything away. I haven't worn any of them."

"That's good, but it doesn't matter," said John. "I'm certain that while she was holding the box she was putting a curse on the jewelry, which already had your energy on it from wearing it. The curse didn't activate until you got involved with another woman."

"A curse?" Nathan sounded incredulous. "I never believed in curses. You mean Kate is responsible for the attacks and the writing on the mirror?"

"Curses are very real," John said. "Yes, it is possible to put a curse on a personal item. The person who owns that item can be affected, even if they are not touching or using it—the curse is linked to your personal energy. Objects, especially personal items like jewelry, are able to hold imprints of a person's energy. It's hard to say if Kate was specific in her curse—she may have just intended for you to never be happy with another woman, and the curse went into effect when you married Nicki."

"Wow." Nathan was quiet. Then he said, "I'm sorry, I'm trying to take this on board."

"No problem. It's a lot, I know."

"So if we get rid of the jewelry, then do we get rid of the curse?"

"It's more complicated than that," said John. "There are spirits that are summoned to carry out curses, and they attach to the objects, and then to a person or place, such as you or your home."

"Oh my God. This keeps getting worse."

"No, things actually are getting better—we know what the problem is now," said John. "Here's what you need to do. The jewelry and the box should be carefully removed from your home, and a spiritual cleansing and binding performed on them."

"Why not throw everything out and be done with it?"

"Whatever is attached to the jewelry needs to be contained," John said. "Otherwise, it might jump to something else around you, and you would still have the same problem."

"How about I send all this stuff to you?" Nathan said. He added, "And I don't want it back, either."

"You can," agreed John. "I know what to do with it. I store a lot of deactivated objects. You'd be surprised."

"I don't think I want to know," said Nathan.

"There's something else you need to do, just to make sure that all the negative energy is out." John prescribed a religious cleansing and blessing for both the newlyweds and their condo.

"You mean an *exorcism?*" asked Nathan, his voice rising. "As in demons?"

"Exorcism is one term," said John. "It doesn't mean you're possessed. It's a spiritual clearing to get any last remaining negative energy." He asked Nathan if they followed a faith or were involved in a church, and gave him recommendations.

The next day, John received a package delivered by overnight express. Inside was the little wooden box and Nathan's jewelry. John did a cleansing and binding on them.

John heard nothing more from Nathan. He let a little time go by and then called.

"Hey buddy, just wanted to check and see how you were doing," John said. "Did you get everything taken care of?"

Nathan told him that a priest came and performed a cleansing and blessing. "We're fine now," he said. "The attacks stopped and we've had no strange activity. No writing on the bathroom mirror. Everything is back to normal, and I mean everything."

John laughed. "I hear you buddy. Okay, that's great. Let me know if anything changes."

"What happened to the jewelry?" Nathan asked.

"It's been deactivated. It's in storage with other former problem objects."

Now it was Nathan's turn to laugh. "You're like a paranormal bomb squad."

"That's a good way of putting it," said John, laughing, too.

"The Asmodeus Curse," Rosemary said when she and John were comparing notes on cases. "Nathan had a lesser version of the Asmodeus Curse."

Asmodeus is one of the most powerful demons in Christian demonology, the demon of lust, jealousy, anger and revenge. Asmodeus originated in ancient Persian mythology, where he was known as Aeshma, one of seven *amarahspands,* which were roughly equivalent to archangels. The early Hebrews absorbed Asmodeus into their demonology, and Asmodeus entered Christian demonology. In various accounts, he was a high-ranking seraph who was among the fallen angels; he was also either the husband of Lilith or one of her demon offspring.

Asmodeus himself was not a factor in the activity, or Nathan and Nicki would have suffered far worse than they did. Major demons have many lesser demons under their control who respond to people bent on revenge, especially when sex is involved. Asmodeus and his demonic horde figure in many possession cases.

One of Asmodeus's legends in the book of Tobit bears a striking similarity to the circumstances of this case. , part of the Catholic canon, was written around the second century BC, originally in Hebrew or Aramaic. The story is complex, and part of it relates how the archangel Raphael, disguised as a man, accompanies a young man, Tobias, on a journey from Nineveh to Media. Along the way, he teaches Tobias how to exorcize demons with the smoke of burned fish heart and liver, and how to heal blindness with fish gall. Raphael also informs Tobias that when they arrive in Media, he is supposed to marry a woman named Sarah, whom he has never met.

Sarah has big problems. The demon Asmodeus lusts after her, and kills any man who marries her on their wedding night before they can consummate their marriage. Sarah has gone through seven men, and now no one wants to marry her. Tobias will be her eighth attempt at a husband.

Tobias is not pleased at this news, but Raphael assures him that he can drive Asmodeus away with the incense of burned fish heart and liver.

Tobias and Sarah marry. When Asmodeus appears in the bridal chamber to slay Tobias, the young man repels the demon with his fishy incense. Asmodeus flees to Egypt, where Raphael captures and binds him.

The curse on Nathan was not as extreme, of course, but it did strike at the wedding bed, and employed dark forces and dark magic to interfere with one of the most sacred of human rites, the consummation of a marriage.

We often see in our work how ancient lore is repeated and played out in modern times, sometimes the same, sometimes with new versions. The old stories contain truth and wisdom still relevant today. The patterns of spirit interference are the same, molded to different circumstances and beliefs.

18

A Chinese Antique With A Zinger

Her name, Jia, was Chinese for "beautiful," and Jia's life reflected her name. Born into a wealthy Chinese-American family, she had grown up with every privilege, including an Ivy League education. She earned a degree in finance and established a thriving and lucrative consultant practice. Her income enabled her to surround herself with luxury and elegance, an independence that she treasured.

Jia was passionate about her Chinese heritage. She loved Chinese antiques and spared no expense when she found something that caught her fancy. Her home was filled with exotic rugs, lamps, pottery, statues, and other rare finds.

One day Jia was browsing through one of the upscale antique stores in town and spied a large figurine of an Oriental woman dressed in a red kimono trimmed in multi-colors. The porcelain was in excellent condition. The figurine was so exquisitely wrought that it looked as though it could come to life at any moment. The woman had a delicate, mysterious look upon her face.

The figurine was expensive, more than even Jia was accustomed to paying, but it called out to her. She bought it without much inner debate.

Little did Jia know that the kimono woman came with an invisible "extra."

Kimono woman joined other figurines in one of Jia's display cases. She admired it every time she walked by.

A few days later, Jia was dusting her collection—she never let the maid attend to her priceless collection of porcelains and ceramics—when an electrical shock shot up her arm. "Ow!" she exclaimed, dropping the feather duster. She looked around to see what could have caused such an effect. Static electricity perhaps?

Jia resumed dusting. As she walked away, another shock went through her. How strange. Was it the carpet?

Soon Jia was getting shocked multiple times every day. She did not associate the shocks with the woman in the red kimono, although they always happened when she was near the case. She took no action, waiting to see if the phenomenon ended.

Then a new complication set in. Jia was beset by migraine headaches. She had rarely had even moderate headaches in the past, let alone severe ones. These monsters put her in bed in agony. The sudden onset of them, as well as their frequency, alarmed her.

Jia wondered if the headaches were caused by the shocking sensations. Her immediate thought was that something physical might be wrong with her. She couldn't pass all the shocks off on static electricity. A physical problem was the only explanation that made sense to her.

But doctors—several of them—were unable to provide answers after many tests. There was no organic cause for the headaches. Stress, they said, advising her to take time off from work.

True, Jia was a workaholic, and often went on streaks of long workdays. This had been a habit of hers for years, however, and she could not fathom why suddenly she should suffer shocks and headaches.

Then Jia made an unsettling discovery: there was a pattern to the shocks, and the only time they happened was when she was near a certain display case—the one containing her new acquisition, the woman in the red kimono.

Still, she thought there had to be a rational, natural explanation. There must be a peculiar characteristic of the figurine that caused such an effect.

Jia went to the case and touched the top of it. An electrical buzz went up her arm. The case had no internal lights, so there was no electrical connection anywhere close that could be responsible. Still, she looked the case up and down and around in search of a cause.

She opened the case and touched each item in it, one by one, arriving at the woman in the red kimono last. All of the items in the case were porcelain and ceramic, and they were all cool to the touch, as normal. But the woman in the red kimono delivered a shock, one stronger than the one Jia experienced when she placed her hand on top of the display case.

Jia yanked back her hand. *What the heck?* Hesitantly, she reached out and touched it again, on the woman's head.

Zing!

She yanked her hand back again. Just to prove the shocks were not a fluke, she reached out and touched the figurine a third time.

Zing!

Jia stared at the figurine. Was it her imagination, or did the woman have a smirk on her face instead of a mystery smile?

Jia staggered backward. Unbelievable! A porcelain figurine nowhere near any source of electricity was delivering shocks to her. What on earth was going on?

Just then her head was stabbed with intense pain. Jia stumbled toward her bedroom and fell across the bed.

When the maid arrived for work, Jia took her to the display case and asked her to touch it. The maid, who spoke little English, shook her head and apologized.

Jia thought the maid was afraid because she had been instructed to leave the items alone in the past. "It's okay," said Jia, pointing to the case.

Still the maid shook her head, looking down at the floor. "No, please not, miss," she said. "No good, no good."

"What do you mean, no good?"

"Bad," the maid said, pointing to the woman in the red kimono. "Bad."

Jia could get nothing more from her that she could understand, due to the limitations of language.

Jia was now totally at sea. She had acquired an object that apparently had the power to deliver electrical shocks and, she presumed, cause ferocious headaches. Nothing in her worldview supported such an idea.

At length she was forced to contemplate some of the superstitions of her cultural background and upbringing, notions that she had always dismissed as the products of backward thinking.

Was the figurine cursed? Jia recalled her Chinese grandmother talking about objects of power.

Nonetheless, Jia never considered getting rid of the figurine. It was too valuable and had cost a great deal of money.

She initiated research on the internet, looking for explanations beyond the ordinary. It was not long before she found John, and gave him a call. Even though his website indicated he dealt in "haunted" objects and was thoroughly familiar with the paranormal, Jia thought he would find her situation hard to believe—perhaps because she still didn't believe it herself.

She was taken aback when he reacted as if zinger figurines were an everyday occurrence.

"In my world, they are not unusual," John said in response to her surprise. He patiently explained how objects can become affected by paranormal influences. He could tell by the energy coming over the connection that, while she was willing to listen, she had her guard up.

"But who would curse a lovely figurine such as this?" Jia asked. "And why?"

"People make curses for many reasons, some of them very strange," said John. "More likely, it is not literally cursed, but probably has a spell on it. It probably holds residual energy from a previous owner, perhaps someone who was very protective of this item. Maybe that person put a spell on it to protect it, which would have summoned a spirit to become attached and guard it. That would explain why, whenever you get close to it or touch it, you get pushed away with a shock."

"The headaches?"

"Many people have different physical effects from being around highly charged objects."

"John, I paid a lot of money for this figurine."

"There are things I can do to clear it," John said. "That may take care of the problem."

"Permanently?"

"It's impossible to make a guarantee," John said. "More than one treatment might be required. If a spirit is attached to the object, we don't want it to get out into the house and attach to something else. I can bring my team in to do an investigation and see what else, if anything, is going on."

Jia made an exasperated noise. "I can't deal with this." Silence. "You know what? Just come and take it away. I positively do not want any investigation. I can't have people tramping all through the place."

John agreed and arranged an appointment.

"This has never happened to me before, in all the hundreds of old things I have purchased," Jia said. "I do not know why this is happening now, but this may be the end of my collecting days." She hung up.

The day before John was scheduled to pick up the woman in the red kimono, he received another call from Jia.

"I've reconsidered," she said, pausing dramatically.

John thought she meant she had decided to keep the figurine and allow an investigation.

"I don't want you to come into the house," she said imperiously.

John raised his eyebrows. Did she think he was going to trail spirits after him like dust on shoes?

Jia went on, "I will have it left for you on the front porch. Come at the time we agreed upon. Take it and leave."

John arrived at Jia's address at the appointed hour. He could not see her house from the road. There was a vast expanse of property behind a locked gate. He pushed the button on the intercom. No one answered, but the gate buzzed open.

John drove down a long, winding dirt road. The house rose into view. It was a huge manor house of brick, with enormous white pillars on the front portico. The grounds were immaculately landscaped.

Oddly, not one living person was about. Wealthy estates were often like that—imposing, perfect, and empty of human presence.

A large circular drive took John to the front steps. There, in a big plain brown shopping bag, he found the woman in the red kimono.

He did not ring the bell, just took the bag and drove off. The gate opened automatically for him to exit.

There was human residual energy and a low-level spirit attached to the figurine. John treated and bound it, and placed it in the Museum of the Paranormal.

He never heard from Jia again.

The case reminded John that the paranormal can strike anywhere at any time, no matter where you live, how much money you have, what you own, what you believe, or your reasons for buying or keeping a particular object.

The Museum of the Paranormal keeps on growing.

19

Advice for Haunted Possessions

How likely is it that anything you bring into your house will be haunted? Fortunately, most people will never undergo the ordeals we've described here. However, everyone sooner or later comes into contact with an item that puts them off or makes them feel uneasy. Eye appeal has little to do with it, for even the most beautiful objects can carry a dark undertow.

Both new and old objects hold energy. A new object can be haunted, but old objects, owned and handled by many people, are more likely to collect troublesome residues and spirits.

Assessing an object

How can you determine whether or not an item is haunted?

Pay attention to your gut reaction
Sometimes we are attracted to certain things because they are unusual, weird, or even ugly in an enticing way. Sometimes we find things that would be "perfect" for décor, a collection, or some other purpose.

Pay attention to your body cues when you look at and hold an object. Whether you realize it or not, you are practicing psychometry, receiving impressions about the object and its history and owners. If the object does not have a good "feel," or if you have any adverse physical reactions, such as a tightening or queasy feeling in the gut, pass on it. There may be no serious problem attached to it, but your psychic radar has informed you that the object is not right for *you*.

In the excitement of a find, it's easy to override or ignore a negative gut reaction. When the item is installed at home, then the adverse reaction becomes noticeable. Rule out normal reactions such as buyer's remorse, or the fact that the object doesn't fit as well as you anticipated. Keep an eye on the item, how you feel around it, and unusual phenomena, if any, in the environment.

Eliminate natural causes

In addition to ruling out buyer's remorse, look for other natural reasons why the environment has shifted in your home. In some cases, we find that people project their personal problems onto the paranormal. For example, marital stress turns into "my spouse is possessed" or "demons are in my house." People also think their houses are haunted after they have watched films or television programs about ghosts. Natural sounds and plays of light suddenly become paranormal.

Paranormal activity does not start without cause, so if you suspect that spirit activity has invaded your house, identify the reason. Consider objects brought into the home near the time the activity started.

Pay attention to the experiences of others

If other members of your household or visitors complain about nightmares, apparitions, or paranormal activity of any kind—and you have ruled out natural causes—take them seriously. Many of the cases in this book feature situations in which the primary experiencer is dismissed or even ridiculed by a partner, spouse, or others. This pattern is common, and actually is no surprise, given the way we are conditioned from an early age in Western culture to regard the paranormal as fantasy.

Disbelieving someone who is under genuine paranormal stress or attack compounds their difficulty, prolongs a bad situation and enables it to get worse, and hinders the efforts of others to provide remedies.

Ignoring the evidence will not make the activity go away.

Remove the object

If you remain uncertain or negative about an object, take it out of the house for a few days and see if there is any improvement.

We have discussed several cases in which people were given cursed objects as gifts. They felt uneasy but kept the objects out of a sense of obligation. The same rule applies: if an object, even a gift, makes you markedly uncomfortable, don't keep it.

It is especially important not to wear jewelry that makes you uncomfortable. Wearing an item deposits your personal energy into it, and also enables a link to be formed between any inhabiting spirit and you.

Remedies

Many objects can be cleansed of low-level residual energy with a variety of methods. Some collectors routinely give their finds a cleansing before admitting them to the house or wearing them; it's a form of "psychic dry cleaning."

Depending on the item and its composition, you can:

- Wipe it down in water containing sea salt
- Sprinkle it with holy water and sea salt
- Place clear quartz crystals next to it
- Leave it out in sunlight
- Hold it and pray over it with a visualization of white light

Get help

When an object has been identified as the cause of serious problems, it is best to consult an expert. If activity worsens in intensity and escalates in frequency, do not wait—get help as soon as possible. The longer activity goes on, the harder it is to end it.

Engage in prayer

Prayer is a powerful countermeasure to unwanted presences. The question is, what prayers are best? Are some better than others?

All prayers are effective. Specific prayers are a matter of faith and personal preference. Every faith has prayers for protection, against evil, and exorcism. Many of them can be readily found on the internet. It is best to use prayers that are meaningful to you, for you will invest them with emotional and spiritual energy.

We caution that for inexperienced lay people, attempting exorcism rites taken from books and the internet is not advisable. You may only accomplish the equivalent of swatting at the wasps and making them angrier. Instead, rely upon the advice and services of religious professionals and clergy.

In general, praying for cleansing and protection, and invoking spiritual help (such as angels, saints, and religious figures) is beneficial.

Dispose of the object
We know of many people who have destroyed, thrown out, or donated haunted objects. Sometimes that ends *their* trouble—but does the trouble itself come to an end? Passing on a problem object means someone else inherits the problem. Improper disposal and destruction may force an attached spirit to latch on to another item, or even a person. This is especially the case with objects that have been used in rituals, spell casting and spirit summoning. The expelled spirit will try to jump to the person who has done the expulsion.

If objects resist remedies, they should be buried in the earth or weighted and thrown into deep or running water. Occasionally John encounters attached spirits who resist being bound, and he disposes of the objects in these ways. Rosemary has used both burial and water immersion in some of her cases, as well.

Personal Protection

Everyone has natural barriers that keep out unwanted interferences, not only from the spirit world, but from the human world as well. For example, people's thoughts and emotions spread out in waves. People pick up on them, depending on how sensitive they are, and spirits pick up on them, too.

An empath is a person who is unusually sensitive to human energy, and is often negatively impacted by such things as anger, depression, and sorrow, the energies of which rub off on them and cling. Such a person could be negatively impacted by residual energy clinging to objects.

Similarly, there are people who are unusually sensitive to spirits, and attract their attention wherever they go. If a dormant spirit is attached to an object, it can be energized to life by a person sensitive to the spirit world.

The natural barrier around you is your aura, an energy field of layers that guard physical, emotional, mental, and spiritual well-being. Some people have thin or weak auras and others have much tougher ones. Auras are weakened by such things as poor diet, stress, illness, certain medical conditions, and recreational substances.

A regular spiritual practice and frequent or daily meditation provide a great boost to the aura. If you have been subjected to detrimental paranormal activity, medical attention and alternative healing may be of benefit. Energy healers can see weak spots in the aura and perform remedial work on them.

Be aware of your own sensitivity to paranormal phenomena. If you are engaged in paranormal or psychic activities, energy healing, or shamanic work, you are more likely to notice or attract spirit attention.

If you love secondhand shopping, don't stop. You may never encounter a haunted object. If you do—you now know how to handle it. In most of our cases, as the stories in this book demonstrate, people had no knowledge of haunted objects and were at a loss when problems occurred. Awareness keeps you ahead of the game.

Resources

More information on haunted objects can be found in the following books and DVDs:

Books

Guiley, Rosemary Ellen. *The Encyclopedia of Ghosts and Spirits*. Third edition. New York: Facts On File, 2007.
_____. *The Encyclopedia of Demons & Demonology*. New York: Facts On File, 2009.
_____. *Guide to the Dark Side of the Paranormal*. New Milford, CT: Visionary Living, Inc.: 2011.
Zaffis, John and Brian McIntyre. *Shadows of the Dark*. iUniverse, Inc., 2004.

DVDs

John Zaffis: The World Within. DVD by Scared! Productions, 2010.

Websites

John Zaffis main website
www.johnzaffis.com

John Zaffis Museum of the Paranormal
www.johnzaffisparanormalmuseum.com

Paranormal Research Society of New England
www.prsne.com

Rosemary Ellen Guiley main website
www.visionaryliving.com

Djinn Universe
www.djinnuniverse.com

About the Authors

John Zaffis

John Zaffis is one of the best-known and most popular authorities in the paranormal. His career of more than 40 years began with working with his uncle and aunt, Ed and Lorraine Warren, noted investigators and demonologists. John was drawn into paranormal investigation and demonology, and gained firsthand experience in cases of hauntings, possession, and exorcism. He has worked with prominent exorcists in Roman Catholic, Protestant, Jewish, and Buddhist faiths, among them Bishop Robert McKenna, Father Malachi Martin, and the Reverend Jun.

John's research has taken him throughout the United States, Canada, England, and Scotland. Over the years he has handled thousands of cases involving ghosts, poltergeists, demonic and diabolical entities, and haunted objects. He has also worked extensively with mediums and psychics concerning the afterlife, spirit communication, near-death experiences, and past-life recall.

John has been featured in numerous documentaries, television shows, and films, among them the Discovery Channel's *A Haunting in Connecticut* and *Little Lost Souls*; NBC's *Unsolved Mysteries, Fox News Live; Piers Morgan Tonight, Ghost Hunters,* and *Ghost Adventures*. For three seasons, he starred in his own paranormal reality show about haunted objects, *Haunted Collector*, on SyFy. He was a producer of the show in its last season. *John Zaffis: The World Within*, a documentary on his life and work, was released in 2010 by Scared! Productions.

John is featured in *The Encyclopedia of Demons and Demonology* by Rosemary Ellen Guiley, and in *Graveyards* and *In A Dark Place*, by Ed and Lorraine Warren and various co-authors. John's first book, his autobiographical *Shadows of the Dark*, co-written with Brian McIntyre, was released in 2004.

In addition, John runs the Paranormal Research Society of New England, an investigation group he founded in 1998. He makes numerous appearances on radio and is always in demand as a presenter at paranormal conferences and at colleges and universities.

Over the years, John has collected hundreds of haunted items in his casework. In 2004, he created the John Zaffis Museum of the Paranormal for the collection. John scripted and starred in a documentary film *Museum of the Paranormal*, released in 2010 by New Gravity Media, which gives a tour of the museum and highlights some of the hanuted objects.

Websites: www.johnzaffisparanormalmuseum.com and www.prsne.com.

Rosemary Ellen Guiley

Rosemary Ellen Guiley is a leading expert in the paranormal and metaphysical fields, with nearly 60 books published on a wide range of topics, including nine single-volume encyclopedias. She has worked full-time in the field since 1983, researching, investigating, writing, presenting, and teaching. Her work focuses on problem hauntings; interdimensional entity and spirit contact experiences of all kinds; "portals" or geographic areas of intense paranormal activity; technological and mediumistic communications with the dead and spirits; the afterlife; angels; fairies; dreams; spiritual growth and development; and psychic skill building. She has done ground-breaking research on Shadow People and the Djinn. She is also involved in ufology, cryptozoology, past-life regression, and reincarnation. She spends a great deal of her time out in the field conducting investigations and research.

In the metaphysical field, Rosemary has studied several modalities of energy healing. She is a certified hypnotist through the International Hypnosis Federation, and conducts past-life regressions. She also does lay dreamwork facilitation, and is a Tarot reader.

Rosemary heads her own multi-media publishing company, Visionary Living, Inc., and produces an e-newsletter, *Strange Dimensions*. She makes numerous radio appearances, and is a frequent guest on *Coast to Coast AM* with George Noory, She is featured in many documentaries and docu-dramas on the History, A&E, SyFy, Discovery, Animal Planet, Destination America, and Travel channels. She had two guest expert appearances on John Zaffis's *Haunted Collector*. In addition, she is a popular speaker at conferences, colleges, and universities.

Rosemary is a consulting editor of *FATE* magazine, and a board director of the National Museum of Mysteries and Research, a nonprofit educational organization in Columbia, Pennsylvania. In the past she served on the board of directors of the International Association for the Study of Dreams, and the board of trustees of the Academy for Spiritual and Consciousness Studies.

Websites: www.visionaryliving.com and www.djinnuniverse.com.